STARTING TO NOD

poems by

Bryan D. Dietrich

Finishing Line Press
Georgetown, Kentucky

STARTING TO NOD

*For John McKenna,
the thunder*

Copyright © 2020 by Bryan D. Dietrich
ISBN 978-1-64662-221-4 First Edition
All rights reserved under International and Pan-American Copyright Conventions. No part of this book may be reproduced in any manner whatsoever without written permission from the publisher, except in the case of brief quotations embodied in critical articles and reviews.

Publisher: Leah Maines

Editor: Christen Kincaid

Cover Art: Arletta Bowlin

Author Photo: Gina Greenway

Cover Design: Elizabeth Maines McCleavy and Nick Greenway

Order online: www.finishinglinepress.com

Author inquiries and mail orders:
Finishing Line Press
P. O. Box 1626
Georgetown, Kentucky 40324
U. S. A.

Table of Contents

The Promise 1

I

78 5
Fatherland 6
The Shape Of the World 10
Passover 16
Let This Cup Pass 22
Love Craft 25
Your Mother's Nakedness 52
Returning To the Ruin 53
Cana 54

II

Drawn To Marvel 57
Alchemy 63
Zombies 65
Lips 67
The Barn 68
The Horde 69
If Only You Could See What I've Seen With Your Eyes 70
Love Poem, Honest 72
Ms. Marvel 73

III

Worlds In Collision 79
Talismans 80
The Death Of Orpheus 81
The Right To Be Forgotten 84
Sea Of Tranquility 86
The Lost Word 87
Raised In the Blood 91
Crossing the Snake 93
The River 102

The Rift 104

*And I will establish my covenant with you;
neither shall all flesh be cut off any more
by the waters of a flood; neither shall there
any more be a flood to destroy the earth.*

—Genesis 9.11

THE PROMISE

My father calls me in to help him rise
from the bathtub where he's fallen. Big.
He's always been big, so much bigger
than the frame that, frail now, has collapsed
in upon him. Gut overlapping what's left
of his hips, snail of a penis shriveled back
into its shell, moles grown vast like lost
continents suddenly found in the thick mist
of tears and shower spew that seem to weigh
him down, my father looks up and asks
what he was supposed to be doing. Nothing,
I say, nothing important, as I raise this man
who raised me back into a world that makes
sense and remember how he used to shake us,
scare us into laundry, long division, love.
How he has hovered over us, infected us,
his voice, his anger, making us mean
more. How he himself means less now.
How this isn't him. How he must have died
years back. How it had to have happened
quietly, artlessly, alone in a strange place,
one he once knew, no family, no fanfare,
no funeral. Later tonight, he will stand
in our foyer, naked again, lost again, looking
for a bathroom, water arcing down legs,
holding himself, ashamed, ancient, new.
I will be ashamed *for* him, for me, knowing
as I do how I've been far too busy with other
things, *important* things. Seven tons of topsoil,
then rain, then mud. Slogging it all, barrow
by barrow, to the back yard. Building berms,
remaking our garden, anything, anything
my Lord, to fight back the flood.

I

In either hand the hastening Angel caught
Our lingering parents, and to the eastern gate
Led them direct, and down the cliff as fast
To the subjected plain, then disappeared.
They, looking back, all the eastern side beheld
Of Paradise, so late their happy seat…

—Paradise Lost

78

Watching his hands vanish into that dark
maw balanced between bake racks,
I stand at the edge of our kitchen counter,
my father bare inches away as he kneels
before the range. Beside me, books. An OED,
a butcher's block of a Bible, the complete
Tolkien. Only the heaviest bindings, weight
to set the crooked straight, necessary gravity.

Earlier, leaving my mother's place, we found it
half escaped from its sleeve in the back window
of our car. Convulsed vinyl, black manta
afloat in summer seat sweat. Anything
else—Cash, Diamond, Clash—we could have replaced,
but this was me, my voice and a hundred others', the All
West Tennessee Choir set down on a 78 some
two hundred west Tennessee parents subsidized.

Now we're back, returned to bachelor's lack, to this
shared flat where he "helps" me with homework,
the table where he's pounded all the math out of me,
yelled until every last digit quakes, till even simple
tasks—dryer time, ratio of Tang to water—
become studies in division. Here, this kitchen
is where I first told him what I wanted
to be. "Writer? Keep writing the shit I've seen so far…"

But now, oblivious to that day he'll find himself
measuring poetry trophies on our mantle,
the one afternoon I'll catch him trying to scale me
to something he can understand… Here,
supplicant at the mouth of the oven, arms
outstretched, hair crisping, skin glossed an angry red…
Neither knows yet what shape it will take or whether,
after, the books will even work. Only this:

He holds the record in his hands.

FATHERLAND

This is a test. Please answer each question
as if you were yourself. Do not forget
to tender a date and name, any name,
in the space provided for your submission.

1. This much you know: The roof is on fire,
rafters raining down like Satan's tinker toys.
A small boy cowers in a closet upstairs.
A Rembrandt, perhaps another Dutch master,
has just begun to peel above the fireplace. Do you:

A. Save the boy
B. Save the painting
C. Hide your shame
D. Choose another life, another dream
 of life where Warsaw was never bombed, where
 the Royal Castle remains intact, where
 libraries lumber ahead unburned, where
 holes were never drilled in your foundation.

2. Imagine all our books, every epic, every
epigraph—*The Father, Brothers, Sons & Lovers,
Little Women, Infinite Jest*, every beloved, satanic
verse, cookbooks, picture books, books full
of phasing, stargazing—imagine them etherized
upon a table, taken up into the Cloud. Remember,
they will be lost, the lot, among plenty. They will
abdicate their authors, be revised, bowdlerized,
trampled, sampled, forgotten. Now, should you:

A. Rejoice
B. Refrain
C. Remain
D. Suspect yourself as obsolete as the forests
 that sustained your quaint obsession, slink
 off underground, invisible, into a cave filled
 with real, solid books and let them burn
 you like a coal mine set aflame.

3. If the *Führermuseum* had been built
in Linz as planned, had all the ill-gotten gilt
the Fatherland got off Jews and Poles and Slavs
been gathered together in Hitler's Aryan Acropolis—
art gallery, opera house, library—if that vast
ballast of emptiness had been filled, what
would it cost to see?

A. Half a million empty walls
B. Six million empty beds
C. One empty sack of saltwater
D. Nothing—the same price one pays for all
    those mummies and marbles, Shivas and divas
    and Balthazars, Indras and Mithras and organ
    jars, all those crystal bones and rosy stones
    that paved the way to London.

4. You are told a Montessori school is closing.
Arriving late, you find almost empty bookshelves,
so much art carted off already, a handful of broken
language records, half a collected set of Vivaldi,
a scratched DVD which told the tale of the planets,
a dog-eared folio on Klimt, some Little Golden guides
to the human condition. When you buy a few
of the latter and leave, do you remember:

A. Your father used to have mad math skills
B. Afghanistan used to have giant Buddhas
C. Hitler painted roses
D. The H.A.L. 9000 computer could sing "Daisy",
    it could take men to the Moon, to infinity
    and beyond, but that was before it had to be
    put down, lobotomized, emptied, data bank
    by data bank, like a mid-sized town in Kansas
    losing its schools, its papers, its Borders.

5. *Your* Fatherland is like Joyland. Abandoned
the way so many sites are abandoned. No joy
left in the rollercoaster's rickets, no fun in the fun
house, the mirrors tarnished, cracked. Even
the scary mechanical clown is a sad shadow
of his former fearsomeness. The disease
that has brought your father to this pass is:

A. Alzheimer's
B. Forty years in the service
C. A bad marriage
D. Too many memories of books and movies,
    and sport, too many artificial experiences
    in a life never lived, never risked, never finished
    the way we see them finished in all those books
    he no longer reads, so had to give away.

6. When they emptied the Louvre, your father
was a young man. He had paintings in him still,
sculptures, wings of victory. He had thirty-seven
convoys of eight trucks each. So much potential.
After the war, after so many wars, after his father
died of dementia, he retired. No more sorties.
No more jets. He sat for decades on the outskirts
of the runway, idling. Did he:

A. Want his art back
B. Want his past back
C. Want his future back
D. Or, like you, did he want his father back, every box
    and crate of him, each ounce of excelsior, every canvas
    finished or unfinished, every winged glory, headless
    or no, pieced from fragments of what had come before,
    every book he kept, his own father's journals, dozens
    of them: "Sat on the bed again today, sat on the bed…"

7. This much you know: Your father is not a museum.
If he is, he has been emptied, ransacked like Krakow.
The *Vernichtung Kommandos* have come and gone.
He sits now in front of you at the Olive Garden. He is
as plain as Raphael's "Portrait of a Young Man," just
as lost. Old. He has grown older while you waited
for your food. Before the food comes, he looks at you.
You wonder if he knows who you are. Are you Poland?
Are you a Jew? Are you that Dietrich from the old show,
Rat Patrol? Have you taken all he has to offer? Given?
Have you given him back all the poems and paintings
he can never understand now? Instead, he asks:

A. Are you my father
B. Do you paint roses
C. Is my father dead
D. Is my father dead and…and you have to decide, do I tell
   him, do I tell him *again*, when he asks *again*, do I lie,
   and *if* I lie, *is* it a lie, and what sort of a lie should it be,
   complex, full of boxes within boxes, or should it be just
   enough to keep the Fatherland running, to keep the trains
   and their boxcars leaving, coughing off down the tracks
   with their horrible cargo, or, finally, should it be lovely,
   the kind of lie that hides the portrait of a young man,
   walls it up, oils it over, the kind of poetry, like paint,
   that preserves the art even though, in the end, it will
   likely never be found again.

When you have finished, please close your books,
place the test in the box, return your writing
implements to their proper place, and remember, this
is only a midterm. You still must prepare for the final.

THE SHAPE OF THE WORLD

I

is a woman kneeling, curved and heavy
breasted, soft as the breath she has to offer,
bringing a brand new body into this space.

The shape of the world is a wailing
infant, bloody and brooding, aching already
to escape this other, larger version

of itself, this mother it will not recognize
until, perhaps, too late. Portal and provider.
Mentor and model. An endless entry

arch whose shadow it will always inhabit.

II

The shape of the world is a kindergarten
class, anteroom to wider wonder, filled
with blocks and bolts of butcher paper,

crayons, crenellated cardboard, a mother
weeping as she drops off her son, sets him
striding into another life, away from her,

from bed and breast and cooking clocks,
her rocker and her shadow box, away,
again away, the same as she ushered him

out the first time, hushed him into being.

III

The shape of the world is a boy bred
on bringing other shapes alive, drawing
whole carnival cavalcades on butcher

paper. Soon, in less than perfect procession,
circus animals, cowboy and commando battles,
cross vast expanses of whiteness, white

as his mother's skin, as the possibility
of failure, as everything she has given him.
They fill the walls of his school like cave

paintings, like blood on a mother's thighs.

IV

The shape of the world is a mother left
alone at home, filling *her* empty walls
with memory, more shadows for her shadow

box, imagining ghosts, all she's lost,
inventing new ways to seal the space
her children have abandoned, this empty tomb.

The shape she imagines does not exist.
The husband she's stuck with does not exist.
The love she seeks is only as real as colored wax,

fabric scraps, her needles and all their points.

V

The shape of the world is a cave in Ardèche
France, a deep, old-world womb thirty centuries
forgotten. It is here, in our infancy, we began

to color the walls with hope and dream, prayer
and fetish, god and monster, self and other.
Here, elk and antelope, ibex and auroch,

rhino and mammoth and bird and bison
run rampant over walls crusted in crystal,
calcite concretions that have not yet erased

who it was we thought we were, or wanted.

VI

The shape of the world for our ancestors
was small, fear-filled, as horrible and haunting
as kindergarten. As lonely as a housewife

alone in Oklahoma, seeking some meaning
from walls that never seemed to end.
What did they desire, these infant artists,

when they braved toxic gas, put hand to stone, filled
that long limestone dark with what animals they could
no longer be, with the relief that comes from hands

dipped in ochre, red as the red that wrought their hearts?

VII

The shape of the world is a handprint left inside
the earth, our Mother. The shape of the world is
a stalagmite erecting itself, up, ever up, into the ark

of the world's womb. The shape of the world
is a mother seeking something to cover her walls—
a sheet tacked over windows, a sheet stained in blood,

an illicit lover whose hands have marked her
skin, make-up to cover bite marks no cave bear
could understand. A wild woman wants what

every woman wants. Power to brave infinity alone.

VIII

The shape of the world is a boy who studies
pyramids, hieroglyphs, cave paintings and comic
books, any kind of sequential art. A boy who

wants a story, any story, to fill each passage
of the silent cave his home has become.
A boy who left elk and antelope, ibex

and auroch, rhino and mammoth and bird
and bison on elementary school walls in order
to own his own dominion, the kind

of labyrinth he could live with.

IX

The shape of the world is a pendant rock
at the back of an ancient cave, at the utmost
anterior, across from a frieze of cave lions,

a stalactite depending from the cave's
curtained ceiling like a giant's penis, rock
carved and painted with symbols that scream

Mother, Other. On one side? The ultimate
woman, bulging pudenda, legs less than
demure. On the reverse? A man with the head

of a bull. Minotaur, sorcerer, secret lover.

X

The shape of the world is a boy grown
to manhood, knowing now how his mother
spent her time in the arms of other men.

The shape of the world is a mother grown
to fit the figure of her ancient madness—
hallucination, depression, dementia.

The shape of the world is an emergency room
where the boy takes his mother to help her hold
her torch just high enough to see what shadows

yet live, what cave bears, what toxins.

XI

The shape of the world is a cave colored in crayon,
a shadow box lit by torch light, a house cacophonous
with carnival carnality, a world beset by beasts,

an empty womb, a lonely labyrinth, a Paleolithic
playground where all the Neanderthals know
the boy knows more…and hate him for it.

He sees their shadows and understands how, if
he draws them, writes them, covers his notebooks
and hard drives with fetishes of all they represent,

he might not cave like his mother.

XII

The shape of the world is an altar stone.
On it, a cave bear skull. Around it, incense.
Beyond, in the deeper dark, a phallus protruding

from above, penetrating the underworld,
carrying life into life. Bull mating with wild
woman. Woman held fast by minotaur.

The image doesn't end at Chauvet. The beast
haunts us still. It haunts the boy, his mother.
She spoke to it that night in the hospital.

She claimed she felt its breath.

XIII

All this art, all this charcoal and chicanery,
all we are, all we've ever been, all we aspire
and fear, revere or find ourselves famished for,

voices echoing in the cave of the skull, ocher
bodies, ocher hands, ocher animals we never escaped,
flower and forget-me-not, blood and shadow

and vision… Is it all our mother? Leaving, left
behind? Or is it simpler? Her death. Others'.
Every grave we drag behind us. What do we want?

A hole in the world in the shape of us.

PASSOVER

I

So it's Passover and Marquez is dead,
his magic gone from the world the way
it's said his mind went toward the end.

And I'm supposed to visit my parents
tomorrow, two hours on the road to ruin,
two houses, two more minds washed up,

washed ashore like the handsomest of dead
men. Last week, Mother called and I tried,
I really tried to hear her. I wanted her to hear

me over her own sobbing. But her ears
access only angels now as she imagines
conversations with vampires and broken

brothers and little dead girls who hide
under the snowdrifts of her Wal-Mart
wardrobe. It's hard enough knowing

she isn't coming back, that, like my father,
she died some time ago, her body yet
moving, her hands still raising stuttering

cigarettes to her lips, but harder still
to keep that phone to my ear while what
is left of her crumples into something

too like incarnate sorrow. She's always
been lost, three quarters of her waking
life spent staring at shadows in a dead

room, dark as the holes in the hands
of Mantegna's dead Christ, but now,
as her days disappear, one by one by one

like her teeth, like the reality she never had
the greatest grip on, the darkness no longer
comforts as it once did. It fills up with her

most insidious imagining. Dead family,
dead children, dead soul. I try to comfort
her, let her know the space between us,

those two hours, are not empty. I can fill
them for her, cross them, come to her, show
her I am not dead, but she can't hear, can't

reason, can't imagine anything isn't eternal.

II

The day after my mother melted down,
my wife called, crying. Another mother,
more distance, more tears. Turns out

she'd seen an accident on her way to work
that morning. And not just any accident.
Terrible. T-bone. Sixty miles an hour.

Big car, big van, glass and scraps of metal
forming a snowdrift on the hood of her
truck. She was the first at the scene,

the first to stop, call 911, the only one
to be there, to hold the hand of the mother
still behind her wheel, strapped in, crying

for the child in the seat behind her. Gina
held her hand, stroked her arm, waited
for the EMTs to arrive, the police, the body

bag for the girl whose face only my wife
could see. One big bruise. Blood, broken
bones. All haloed by blonde hair, Hello

Kitty hair barrettes. Gina had to wait
with the woman for fifteen minutes, wait
for the experts who would lift the little

girl into their arms, onto the gurney, slide
her into the back of the ambulance like someone,
surely someone, slid Christ into his tomb.

The door closed. The woman was taken
away. And Gina, my wife, mother of our child,
left standing, staring into the sky, remembering

every dream she'd ever had, every nightmare
of our son found dead, found bleeding, found
impaled or drowned or strangled or beaten,

crushed or sickened, abducted or eaten.
And now, calling me, crying, unintelligible,
as far from her husband as my mother was

from her son, grief washing over all that absence,
all that distance, the way Mary's hands must have
caressed Christ's skin, cleaning him, holding him,

soaking in the sorrow of her only seed.

III

About suffering, they were slow
to understand, the old Masters. So
much distance between dying Gaul

and dying Christ. All that empty air filled
with the sound of hammers and altars,
rising and falling wings, rising and falling

empires. Thermopylae, metropoli, necropoli.
The sound of so many mothers crying.
After the purges and plagues and burnings,

after the invasions and collapse, before
notes nailed to doors or sectarian schisms,
before even more dead children, a little space,

a little season emerged for them to listen.
Cimabue resurrected emotion, Giotto,
the weight of the real. All those Vans?

Eyck, Goes, Weyden? So much detail,
perfection, the dark textures of reflection.
Masaccio, he who provided all we needed

for perspective. And then Mantegna, coroner,
homicide detective, exhibiting the body
of Mary's brown-eyed boy. Plain, unadorned,

simple as supper. And Duccio, Ghirlandaio,
Angelico, Filippo Lippi, each addressing
that mother who knows her child must die.

Botticelli's Madonna taking comfort from
the classical, from Persephone and her fruit,
the hope her seed might sprout again.

Veneziano offering up St. Lucy's eyes. Da Vinci
and Raphael following suit, seeing the need
to focus on a middle ground, not what lies ahead,

not the sfumato of sorrow where we lose ourselves
in fog and break upon the rocks like our Lady,
that dark, formless void where only Michelangelo,

most terrible of the old masters found the right
shape, the cold stone contours of every Mother
and her fear. Dead child, distant as a hill of skulls,

silent as a snowdrift. One last lie upon her lap.

IV

Yesterday, Gina's mother called, crying.
Another death. This time her mother's brother,
the one she all but raised. More distance,

more tears tearing the fabric of space and time
across miles and miles, all the empty spaces
between Kansas and California, between

mother and child, child and clouds of glory.
Did Da Vinci, did Michelangelo know
what it means for death to pass us by?

Is this why my own mother cries, wishing
it were her, not everyone else? Wishing
it was finished, done, over, no more

hammers tacking sheets over windows,
beating nails into walls and coffins and hands?
No more voices from afar. No more

annunciations, golden words laying
gilt across her vision? Is this why Mary
left us, left the world without leaving

her body? Had she had enough of death?
When the spirit of the Lord came to take
all those desert children, all those dusty

lives… When the bloody finger of a God
steeped in plagues tried the doors
of every family in Egypt, took each child

whose parents had not bathed their own
hands incarnadine, who had not flushed
their thresholds with the red that rises,

engorges, makes us larger, more open,
allows us to make more of ourselves…
When the angel of death left the firstborn

strewn across the fertile crescent in pale
pink snowdrifts, and morning came
and the lamb had saved the rest, which mothers

leaned over their cribs like Mary over the dead
Christ in the Pieta? Which wondered,
has my child risen? Which, is my child dead?

Which knew, then, there could be no end to asking?

LET THIS CUP PASS

I

The man sits on his bed, one hand holding
a plastic cup, the other, the place
where his leg came off. His sheets smell
of bad Spam, of frogs baked to oblivion
by the sun. His other leg isn't long
for this world. He only leaves his trailer
twice a week now, once for groceries,
once for the liquor that lets him stay here
in his bed, in his underwear, in the dark
broken only by what little light can stab
its way in, between his broken shades.

But that's not entirely true. There *is* more
light, emerald and onyx, alive with the kind
of reflected glory he used to see in the cisterns
he built, the skies he stood beneath, daring
the twisters to come. He was a man of his hands
then—plumber, carpenter, mule skinner, even
built swing sets for his grandchildren from old pipe
and tractor parts—but now he simply sits
and sips, his Zenith's green twisting different
shapes from gangrenous sheets, the haze of Pall
Malls and Schenley's Black Death, his hands

too unsteady to tame the seething storm.

II

The painting presents a horizon of hubris
and horror and hate, armies advancing toward
the mangle of mill wheels, houses and churches
aglow with the light of their own burning, lost
souls seeking doorways into flame. It lurches
then, below these surfaces, into another
world where ghouls garrote victims, drag them

to spits and gallows, where everyone, where we
break beneath the weight of great severed ears
or march as cannon fodder for secret insect wars,
where we are used as bait, fed to mutant birds

and cannibal cats, where we are forced to swim
in filth, vomit up entrails, serve as place settings
for mad March hares, or as cold concubines
to horny, habit-wearing swine. Here,
in this place below all places, beneath all
our earthly delights, we are servants to each
inbred impulse Bosch knew already makes us
mean. Here, we are nothing more than cat-gut
strung on the bones of harps we've forgotten
how to play. Here, where ruin rages—black
above as below—the animals we once were

swallow us like the plague we have become.

III

My sisters used to read me horror, fearsome
folktales from a book called *Strangely Enough*.
Late nights, at Paw Paw's house, shuddering
beneath sheets, they fed me sip after sip
of history's black broth, stories simmered
on the stove since long before the first pox,
tales to turn a childhood white. Black tales
of the man with the golden arm, the ghost girl
in blue velvet, the story of the white dove
with red breast that sat season after season
upon a certain, graveyard, snowball bush.

Tales of misshapen mists, fiendish footprints,
cobalt colts, and a yellow window gone black,
only once each year, in an ancient oil
on an ancient wall. The whole color wheel

of whips and racks and rats, funeral hacks,
the plague's black axe, high keening in the woods
when the night goes green. This was before Paw
Paw's decline, before he lost his legs, before
divorce found its way into his world and our own.
What were we doing then, after gloaming, beside
ourselves, telling old tales deep into the long dark?

What, if not preparing for the fall?

IV

Bosch knew about my grandfather. He saw
my mother holed up in her dark room, saw
my father crying on his son's slim shoulder,
my sisters, me, stuck with absent lovers season
upon season, white doves, red breasts, soldiers
in an army of insects, the flea that infects each
heart with war. Like Dante, like Lady Bathory,
like the Borgias and their cups, secret
compartments in the handle, like every poison
that lingers in our grasp, Bosch knew it all
begins in the garden, in the bush, in the shade

of that pink tree, both fountain and phallus,
ossuary and ovary, how we climb from one
pit only to descend to another. He understood
the organs we play, how they play *us* to decay,
how we wind up, winded, in a bag, on a table,
in the morgue, cold and alone and how—
when the carpenter comes, he who would make us
swing again—how we find ourselves alive again,
always again, but only for the shortest spell.
How do we die? How do we kill ourselves?
How, let the world burn? Just this. And this.

Another this. Another cup of darkness.

LOVE CRAFT

> *The fascination for the historical past we might
> interpret, in Lovecraft, as a profound wish that
> the present might not yet have happened...*
> —Joyce Carol Oates

I. NECRONOMICON

First, feel the itch. It will begin like sin,
a growing glass glissando down your bones.
Next, wander your halls, a haint haunting familiar
rubble, this embarrassing stubble stumble
of standing stones. Ignore doors, swelling floors,
seek the catacombs. Now, find your enclave,
your cave, that library you've lined in shadows
from the grave. Dead words only alive
as long as eyes allow, as long as lips
crave. Next, peruse the staggering stacks,
reach for what attacks your fancy and draw
it down. Fear the possibility you find
there, yes, but notice the embossing, the gentle
spindles of what once might have been
thorns, now simple *fs* and *ps*, never enough
es. Fondle the spine, feel how it breaks
in the space where leather meets leather.
Lover, tether. Listen. Can you smell it?
History. Remember that it cannot *not*
contain that place where you will end. Imagine,
though, what might ensue. Take the risk. Do.
Tell. Open the book, brace yourself, say the spell.

II. HE

*A man rises to the surface, silent
and dangerous in the dark, his second
skin sleek as an Oxford oil slick. Mounting
to the dock, he pockets his prototype*

microlung and seeks the shadows to unzip.
Water laps at the pilings, a loon calls out,
scuttling clouds make the moon specter.

Drawn in too close, an unlucky guard
finds his neck noosed, his body snatched
kicking into darkness. We hear nothing
of the struggle, just the sound of a zipper
as the man—now dark dove in a crisp white tux—
ducks away from the dock, his abandoned
wet work, only to ascend some nearby steps.

A path. A garden party. Behind him
in the harbor a ship explodes, dignitaries die,
plans for some sort of pan-global conquest sink,
and our hero, snipping a single flower
from the hibiscus bush with a dead
man's boot knife, freshens his lapel—a touch
of Eden—then glides into dinner all aglow.

My father's watching secret agent movies
again. All car sparkle and roulette rattle.
Flying tank tackle, knife flourish, dish swish,
Beretta flash, Euro-trash, secret satellite
metal battle. Ditch crash, requisite lust
rush, adrenaline flush, walkie-talkie tattle,
and the idle gargle of embargo prattle.

From my own secret stash of plastic drastics—
toy time bombs, Walther P.P.K.s—my deep sea
pillow cave constructed near my dad's recliner,
I watch the light of our Zenith fade,
crest, then fade again across his face,
the silhouette of a retired jet pilot
thrown large, edges unresolved, upon the wall.

He's told me all the stories, not-so-tall
tales of private aerial shows over his home
town, of flying sleek steel under thunder
heads the size of the Isle of Man. I've seen pictures
of him, a diamond in formation, pressed
wing to wing, content to plow a plane-sized hole
right next to four others. Any time. Any mountain.

Even that eerie-eyed shot I keep in my room—
black and white, flat top, colonel crop in full dress—
seems to follow me. Afternoons, while I wait for him
to clock off from a job he does by number
now, his latest government DOS crisis, cubicle
Rubicon... While I deck our bachelor walls with penlight
laser sensor, kite string trip tensor, he watches.

The father that returns to me now is not
this other. At eleven I know this, know the man
who could land a plane, engines aflame, in fog
thicker than Mother's flap batter, the father who flew
through Cadets younger than all who filed through before,
who cake-walked high school at fifteen, *that* father is not
the one who'll trip my traps, spy spats boobied by the door.

Next night—after row on row of aughts, after Clue,
after bologna and sugarless tea, after bikes
and bills, the weekly ledger badger where he sits
me down and pencil whips me with all we owe—
we go back to our book, the one we left off last
evening, the real deal, not Connery or Lazenby
or Moore, and begin *You Only Live Twice* again.

Thing is, the books' hero isn't that debonair
hair-care ad we see on screen, M's grim machine, never
shaken, rarely stirred swagger with a smile, high tech tool
kit who arrives on cue. Rather, on *paper*, he's little
more than glorified pen pusher, a senior civil
servant who, tops, adopts the double 0 only
thrice a year, counting down to death before forty.

This man is dry, depressed, a bit stale, pale grey
suit among green, the dull sheen of cabinets,
parliament habiliments, piles of files.
Clock tick and ticket tally. Not rocket docket,
but the grind's blind alley. A fragment of a man,
fit only for shadows, the occasional affair.
So, a rogue *cum* commando, commander of flair...

That, or silhouette... These are the Bonds we share.

III. THE NAMELESS CITY

i

First it was the Painted Desert, its striated
sands plum purple and incarnadine, a blood
plump sun hemorrhaging on the horizon.

Next, the Petrified Forest, even emptier
for having been green once. All sap stopped.
All bark, bone. Splendor, yes, but glass.

Add to these the Grand Canyon, our most famous
vacancy, a ghost town teething its tombstones
to nubs, the great Arizona crater hollow as a crib

death. Then the Mojave, the sad soughing
of a thousand windmills. All the abandoned
places in the earth. It was our first summer after

the divorce, a Brady Bunch special without
any lovely Lady, and I guess we needed
something—comfort, closure, claustrophobia—

anything to do again as a family.
My father, me, my two youngest sisters, one
brand new seventy-seven Monte Carlo...

By the end, we'd sprung a door, stripped the faux
leather top, made the trunk uninhabitable with decaying
sand dollars, the dead skeleton of a star. My father

had slapped one sister by then, alienated both,
taught me how not to live. But before all that,
one Tuesday along the way, grey rain calling

its sister mist up from the earth, Daddy
coaxed us free from cloud-fed ennui, our room's sole
console, and we left the *Twilight Zone* behind,

parted from *Dark Shadows* only to arrive
at Bedrock, a forgotten TV park tie-in.
Last stop before the happiest place on earth.

ii

Homes harrowed out of hornblende, vast slabbed
roofs of sandstone, doors of lime, foundations
of feldspar and gypsum. We wiped our feet

on chert and entered the Pleistocene cartoon
hut by cartoon hut, visited each damp hogan
alone. No other Okies to accompany our slide

back to the simple, nothing but fading screens
imbedded in the walls. Old episodes
of the *Flintstones* airing endlessly for no one.

Halfway through the self-guided tour, cattywampus
from the only brontosaurus there was
to climb, almost even with a giant snake hollowed

for the swallowed (those who could best imagine
being gone), one step behind my family, finally
I began to fall further back, noticing cracks

in our amusement. Chicken wire, plaster. All that seemed
so sad, even sadder now. What had started out
fake, what we'd classified as at least kitsch, now lost

even that little luster. Everything here, all that was meant
to be boulder... All falling apart and only us as witness.
In the end we wandered back to the car, silent. Not a soul

spoke for miles. We suspected he'd brought our mom
here once. Perhaps she'd been addicted to the damned
cartoon. *Maybe*, he said, *maybe she can join us*

next time. Still, we didn't speak. To this day I can't
forget that second silence, all the broken, rocky
homes, each inch of dead air. Even now I think

if you opened my father's head you'd find a stone
age chimp, chisel and granite slab in hand,
hammering away at his idea of love.

IV. THE WHISPERER IN DARKNESS

I used to take great pleasure in stabbing
it, his chair, working a pen or cast off
purling needle into its side. The feel of steel
sliding into Naugahyde, the first, tough
pop through taut surface into an imagined
interior where so much lay empty

was just too sickly satisfying to stop.
Of course I kept my furniture murder
secret, on the side, next to the wall
in a cushion-sconced crawlway meant only
for me, a surrogate coffin-slash-club
house where I coveted everything monster.

Late night, amber Sunday afternoons,
my father beside me, I would lie
there between his world and my own
and watch our color console divide us, all
of us, into black and white. Sometimes
it was sacrifice—Karloff's Im-Ho-Tep
incanting Zita Johann onto his slab.
Sometimes revenge—*The Black Cat*, Lugosi
skinning Karloff the way they say he always
wanted. But other horrors dissected us
differently: *The Blob* made men mob, *Frogs*,
only too human, and Ray Milland as X?

His freakish vision's reach preached limits
for our dream, the unseen, what must remain
beyond the caul. But our most common
parsing came under influence of the moon.
Valerie Gaunt, Ingrid Pitt, Isobel Black.
Blood-suckers over and over again. *Daughter,
Brides, Scars of Dracula*. Both Universal
and Hammer. *Lust for, Lovers of...* All vampires,
daughters of darkness, all blood and roses.
Dark power, dark women, so much lurid loss.
According to my father, the one that scared him
most was *The Vampire Bat*. He was ten.

No dad to watch with, no chaise to deface.
Returning from the Bijou, one final chore
before bed, on the way to the creek, he freaked,
ran screaming back to the house. What was it,

down in that gully, too near the unmoving
black flood? Was it fear of something coming
or something already arrived? Fear of the black
or that lack that it implies? Even at ten myself
I think I recognized the way Mother used him,
the way he let her. So much stuff—pumps, pants
suits she'd never wear, two tomb-sized boxes
of fabric bolts, all the graveclothes she'd never need.

His sisters also. By now they've nearly
broken him. Bad boyfriends, bad broods,
bad brains and fading hansoms. Women,
always women. One sister who stole Mother's
rings, another who frenzied him into a freezer
for *her* dam... Why did he love them? Why
still? He told me once he used to tend the church
lawn. Later, at fifteen, the cemetery too.
Those days, from my corner covey, from there
or on his belly, watching my first horrors,
I wondered what it must have been like,
mowing the uncut hairs of graves.

Bewitched by Wacky Packs, by the Wonder
Bread creature card series, each with tortured taglines,
stats on the back, bewitched but transfixed, watching
my father watch from his chair, it seemed I saw
him there, a shadow between the deeper shades
of sod. Did he shudder, imagine more than the simple
implications? He loved, still loves horror. But
did he have to cut them all, even, say, his mother's
monthly nettles? She died when he was three.
Tornado. She was pregnant. *He* was in the field
almost a mile from their shack, from the dark
cellar hold she'd have believed their only

hope. She filled that gap between them in less
time than it took, later, to lose his youngest
sister, Charlotte, born dead. And she, Lessie?

Dead of hemorrhage before she could shake
that stitch in her side, the burn in her legs,
my dad's dead weight in her arms. Of course
back in TV time, during those blood feasts
brought to us by Tang and Cross Your Heart
bras, during the quiet moments when I'd lose
interest in both bad movie and my botched bat
attacks, coffin deconstructions (what *was* I
doing?), back then, he never said her name.

Today, he sits in the same chair, retired,
reading mysteries, monster disasters, sci-
fi. It's almost as if he's never moved. Mother
still lives with him. They're divorced. She pays
rent now. And, God help them both, he still loves
her. There's even a quilt at the foot of the thing,
a pillow near its scars. He naps there. Breathing
problems. Can't sleep. Perhaps part of it
is the money, all the blood he's attempted
to buy; perhaps his sisters', lovers', others'
knack for never ponying up; perhaps poverty
as he sees it coming. This, or the dreams.

One night, not long ago, he says he felt
something crawling up from the floor, up
onto his feet, up shin and thigh, toward the high
belly he's grown from years of sitting still.
He began to kick, to yell, woke bruised
and bleeding, sunk deep in a skeleton
of combed metal, winged arms, the faux
infinity of comfort zones, this chair
where, before I left it to attempt to kill it,
I learned to love loss, dross, all those gloss
embossed blood junkies who carry us
out of ruts, into holes, and keep crawling back.

He owns a stone now, a funeral plan, a plot,
but hasn't come down on a coffin. His father

never spoke of it. His family...well...what is this
heaviness, forgiveness? What does it mean
to not let go? Why do we need to practice
puncturing hearts? Forgive me, but finally,
what's at stake? Vampires? Who tends their graves?
I love my father. I love my family. But I could
no more say this in a poem than he could
say it to any of us. He's always been cold.
He *could* cut the grass. He could lay down on her
and weep. No one teaches us to be alone.

V. COOL AIR

Every day. In deluge. In delight. His chair.
He has worn the form off of it. It is not so much
anything as him. It smells of Old Spice and Brut.
It wears its hair short, crop-topped, save for the fall
from the back that feels forward over that tell-tale
blankness, reaching toward eyes that are no longer
eyes, lids no longer lids, locking out nothing now,
a mind no longer mind but mush, made of the stuff
that stuffs the TV set it sits before. My father, the chair,
leans back into his life, listing. Snow, rain, a front
coming in off the Rockies. My father, the chair
could have been a weather man, chose vacuum
tubes instead, punch cards instead. He could have
been Oklahoma's Gary England, stormwatcher,
tornado chaser. Chose Air National Guard over air,
programmer over program. Now he is the program.
He no longer wonders whether this is even okay.
My father, the chair, is in recline. He could, retired
now, go anywhere in the world for free, hop a plane,
head out for Hungary, Calgary, Calvary, anywhere
where he isn't a chair, but then he knows too much
about what the weather is like out there, what he might
miss, here, alone before the altar of his unction.

He might not be here to see the weather change,
the channel change, the sign off, all that snow.

VI. THE UNNAMABLE

Each day it comes to take a tiny bit more, not so much
what he has or has had—this he is allowed to savor
still—but it takes what never was, what he could never be.
The astronaut's dream, that one shot, years ago, at galling
both gravity and God. Weather man? Full Colonel? Gone.
Gone, too, the good wife, the love he could have lived
with another—young, old, lovely, wise. A woman for whom
one world might just have been enough. Better children, fonder
memories, friends. More pool, more poker, another ragtop
ride though Honolulu. Even jetlag, a war wound perhaps, more
hurt, more skirt, more time with his mother before she died.

But all of this fades along with the words he would need
to express regret. Like a madman fresh from the rain
in some space-eater saga, some Lovecraft legend, he's lost,
lingering only long enough to explain how he *can't*
explain why. All those Robert E. Howard books, our hero
humping his way between horrors… All Ashton Smith's
smithery, Long's longing… Each tome in his lumbering
library, every colour out of space… These fail too.
It's not that he doesn't read anymore, no, he swallows nearly
a novel a day, but now that it has come to take what *isn't*
away, he simply can't keep up. Wilbur Whateley, warped.
Dexter Ward, deleted. Pickman and his models, all washed
out. And as he begins them once again—re-encountering
each old god, each reach for that which lies behind the darkness
behind stars—even now, none are the least bit familiar.

And tomorrow? Today's pages will flock its narrow nest.
It isn't what one might imagine—Cthulhu, Ubbo-Sathla,
some ghost from another time, another plane—no. No

Necronomicon, no *Lost Book of Eibon* has called it
into this world through cracks between betweens.
Whatever has come, what continues to feed, what takes
from him all he ever wanted—that negative space that makes
a man mean—it drinks his dreams, his books, his words
away. It leaves no solids, no nouns, only pronouns,
vague phrases, incantations of loss as he sits and stares,
trembles with two final, horrible words: he's happy.

VII. FROM BEYOND

That year my wife who neither of us knew
would be my ex wanted a crystal ball.
Six years before the divorce, five before
the calm, four before the silence, before
the yelling before that—Kansas and moving
truck…hell, a whole Halloween wedding not
even on our radar yet—before the secrets
and skirmishes, diary dervishes, before my guilt
and her lack, I stood, poor, white, trashed, surfing
the bric-a-brac shelves in Dillards, plastic
play money burning holes in both my pockets
and our future, looking for a lens to let
her know just how deeply we'd descend
before breaking. I hadn't expected
to find what she wanted, but unable
to afford the real thing from, say, Voyager's
Dreams, House of Shadows, I'd backed myself
into this, the softer side of Sharper Image.
Trying to decide between one oracle ovary
and the next, I caught a woman, inverted,
reflected in my would-be prize, coming up
the aisle, her boy, maybe five, tear-assing
between marble tissue box covers and consoles
so small they looked like two-way wrist TVs.
After he'd barked his shin on the inevitable

glass shelf, after his mother leaned down,
began rubbing the wound, chanting, *Blood
of Jesus, blood of Jesus*, I found myself
sprinting through the rabble of augury baubles
faster, faster, afraid she— *You know you
won't find Jesus in a crystal ball*, she said,
suddenly beside me, eyes as round as the spheres
only she could hear. Flustered, I turned away
and found, instead, another aisle, one with other
kinds of orbs, globes, a model of Mars, Earth,
some sepia tone. I haven't a clue why I settled,
but walking out with this unintended present,
one so much larger than what I'd dreamed, I flashed
on the sign that used to squat on my home
town Baptist lawn: *You won't see God with any
Hubble*. It was almost Christmas. I couldn't tell
what lay in our future. I didn't know
what would happen in Kansas. I just took
the world, tottering in its box, and headed home.

VIII. AT THE MOUNTAINS OF MADNESS

The air is thin and I'm starting to nod.
Through the open window, the smell of pine
and deer velvet, the wet fust of beaver
tooled aspen, birch bitten with a touch
of frost, mingles with a young boy's breath,
the lingering perfume of dreams coming on.
Here, twelve thousand feet and change above
sea level, locked in love between wife
and son in the back seat sweat of my in-law's
4 x 4, I begin to lose my way. These woods
we wander—switchback by switchback, climbing
rockfall, bounding down Dantean brook bed—
the epileptic shiver of steel tire
over shale, seem to rock me out of one

life into another where I am mining
the silver they once pulled from these purple
pulpits, the life blood of Big Red Mountain.
I am no longer poet, professor, but the Hermit
of Stony Pass, my heart so full of shafts,
the precious buried so deep, each rill that rolls
back down to the Rio Grande runs bloody
with rust, with iron, all I've mined to get
to the heart of what I might be losing.

Before we left, my mother asked for help
designing her second tattoo. At sixty
six, she wants a heart to go with her
Hairstreak, wants I ♥ U MOM in red
over her ribs, wants those who open her
up to believe someone did. And on the way
here, passing that mountain, we saw a mudslide,
trees savaged from the sierra in the shape
of love's vaginal ideal, a perfect valentine,
its gaping absence pulsing just below the line
where air gives out. When we come to the stand
of birch we're looking for, three generations
piling out of that Ram, as I take the blade—
scrimshaw hart on its handle—in hand
and begin to carve yet another heart
beneath the open scabs of so many
earlier operations, as I join this family,
having left so much of my own behind,
I think about Cain, the seal he was
sent to bear, about my newest love, the son
we now share, and the stain they found, just this
June on a plate of heaviest metal, a stain
the mercury marked, still marks, on her map.
East of her heart, then left, then morning.

IX. THE SHADOW OUT OF TIME

i

My mother's reflection in the polished red
oak turns clockwise like a ghost against
the grain, and at the juncture of lid
and lip begins to bleed into satin. Fenced
in by steel, by granite, rope and wood,
by family, these shadows carved from wind,
she traces her brother's veins once ripe with blood
to pluck the rigor mortis from his hands.

Her breasts believe in Christmas, though the rose
she bears between them and the hard December
leather of her coat does not remember
how to open in the dark, at funerals
where stones will still be stones tomorrow,
where blood and silver stop the pump at zero.

ii

This house grows smaller with each pulse
that's taken from it, each reception
in the kitchen where once worn chairs converse
with air. She knows these walls have one direction,
out, that clothes still line the closets, wings of black
witch moths pile up in fixtures, rusted grills
of coolers rudely weather-stripped with sacks
and cellophane.   She fingers a doll whose frills
have yellowed, whose drawn heart has dissipated
in sulfur, the smell of piss and ink.
Raggedy Andy no longer blinks,
his eyes unbuttoned. She cinches his pleated
coat to hide what missing chambers she once filled
with all these strangers' faces unrevealed.

iii

Sitting in a corner of the dark
room, Mother's sisters mill the smoke she breathes,
discussing how their brother couldn't work,
so long connected to a plumber's dream
of tubes. How eyes, unraveling in their pits,
began to wander in the grayer matters
of time where she and he were sticks
together, bundled in a mattress
when the dust began to curl, its edge
silent as the clouds unearthed the power
of the sky, hail clawed the tin for hours
and shook the chimney from its brooding age

to bed springs so unlike the ones
where death and he made love. Her shudder comes.

iv

They played together, lovers of the field,
potatoes grown from eyes beneath their heels.
The dust was something children did not yield
to, though her father cursed the sun, its wheels,
its wagon ruts that notched his brain
like irrigation. Sometimes in the whispers
of the clock, beneath the sheets, she spoke of pain,
fathers, liquid shame, large slippers
approaching her bed.   Her brother cried
for her and held her to his chest, already
shrinking from the insulin it hurried
to digest before the crops began to die.
She ate potatoes every night, dined
on roots that later withered two from nine.

v

Though her brother lost his eyes between
family, feuds, depressions, diabetes
did not insulate *her* world. She's seen
her sisters turn by slow degrees
toward the sun, toward the death that comes
from ruts beneath a heat she cannot bear.
Unlike them, she's picked the midnight bones
for life that does not sell its sight to hear
the prayers of garden gods, sick, sad, greening.

Save the oldest one, the sister she won't name,
who stole her from her marriage with a lame
attempt at love. Faye seasoned her with dreaming,
gave her lust for gold and silver, myrrh.
Mother isn't like the others aren't like her.

vi

Faye called her when she knew their brother's
heart was sizing boxes for the field,
digging memories to plant beside another
wall. She blamed my mom for distance, concealed
lust, money she could not give, a liver
too notched with a dead father's ghost.
Sitting in the house *her* mother never
means to leave until the wind is lost
in six more stones, Mother holds the ragged doll,
bears her sister's pouting, parting kiss,
thinks of potatoes and blood and Judas
and clutches her dress.
                                    The rose is there, is all
that isn't rooted in her heart or other
coffins than her father's, husband's, brother's.

X. THE THING ON THE DOORSTEP

What is it she's afraid of? Living in the dark,
blankets thumbtacked to the sill along each pane,
my mom sits and smokes and watches the Discovery
channel next to a lineup of the usual suspects.
Porcelain dragons, clone after clone of Betty
Boop, a carnival glass heart, its aperture clogged
with littler clutter, empty lighters, two plastic
poodles, one white, one black, attached to opposing
magnets. Here, a row of mug shots, me, my sisters,
Mother's sisters. There, a diorama of the lost
toys from some wooden Christmas classic.

The light filters in, but only in seizures, setting
airborne tobacco ablaze. One frame—split,
sectioned off for photos, individual tin types
and serigraphs—oversees it all, its single
empty eye taking my mother in. Aunt Sissy,
upper right. Aunt Joy, Aunt Carol, more toward
the center. And there, to the left, the sinister
side of things, a hole. Aunt Faye hasn't inhabited
that space for many years now, not since she called
my dad, clued him in to Mother's more obscure
outings. She calls this sister Momma's daughter.

Once, I made the mistake of pointing out the way
they favored one another. She went off on Faye's
own infidelity, to her, said it was spun
from spite. But I remember Faye's lawyer
husband, Henry. Then *my* dad, National Guard.
Their house, better, brighter. *Their* car, always
bigger, blockier, leather crisp as fresh cash.
Last month Mom called, said the witch was dead,
blew herself up lighting a Salem in her oxygen
tent. I didn't go to the funeral, didn't figure
she would either, but she did, came back sick.

Now she sits in her room again, still watching
the show. Some astrophysicist talking about tears
in time, about two circling anomalies "locked
in a death dance." He asks, "Is this pair of black holes
an old married couple, or just strangers passing the night?"
Mom still lives with Daddy, rents a room. I've said this
before. She uses him, he uses her. Her sister used
them both. I remember the divorce, back when Faye
was still a worship word, when she came and offered up
her husband for free. That's when she gave my mom
those magnets. I used to play with them, pushing one

forward, watching the other turn, flip, attempt escape,
flip again, come running. The physicist won't stop
spewing. He's discussing dark matter now, how
more than ninety percent of everything isn't
even there. Either in our cells or in the stars. Empty
space, empty ashtray. My mother takes the ashes
that have accumulated in her coffee can, walks
to the garage and—passing my father asleep in his chair,
a book about starships balanced on his belly—
enters the cool dark between the bodies
of their cars. She dumps her filters, all the fragile

arms, all those eroding, orbiting skulls of gray.

XI. THE LOVED DEAD

i

My mother has always envied the dead.
One night at supper she explained how
she didn't want anyone undressing her
after, how she preferred ash to cherry.

Later, when I was nearly ten, she served
notice to my father: *I'd do it now, but
what would the kids find? How would they heat up
their breakfast, my nightgown caught in the broiler?*

I remember her locked in her room, weeks
at a time. We'd bring her ice water in plastic
cups, dole out her pills for her, make sure her bell
clapper wasn't strangled in its own chain.

Then the *truly* black moods, naked, rocking
back and forth on the bed, knees to her chin,
a doll or bear or gnome clutched to her chest.
In the corner, her terrariums, weeping.

ii

Recently, she's taken to reminding me
of what she expects. The first half must be
divided up between my sisters. Of the rest,
half goes to Daddy—credit cards, rent, her

lust for black hills gold. After that, what's left
is mine. And her body? Science. She's always
said she didn't want anyone laughing at her
"tiny titties," didn't want some undertaker

undertaking, well… The weird thing is, I
imagine her intended audience much larger
than any wake. Students, graduate assistants,
lab techs, poking, peeling, removing at last

that unformed twin laced to the base of her spine.
I invent macabre keg parties in some juco Lurch lab,
young, drunk coeds playing Spin the Skull, Operation
Orgy, or zipping her up for room for Hearts.

iii

Today is July 11, her birthday. My new
wife and son and I are headed down to Moore
for what I know will likely be less. Earlier,
on the phone, she said, *This is it. The last hill*

I'm gonna climb. She said she'd shoot herself
beneath her left breast if she didn't know
she'd hurt her kneecap. That's my mom.
We're driving down anyway, trying to catch up

with homework on the way. I'm tutoring Gina
on poets, confessionalists, deep image subjectivists,
Bishop, Lowell, Plath, Sexton, "The Broken
Home" by Merrill. She wants to know why,

in Rich, every woman's a wreck, why, in Dickey,
the woman has to fall. Why, among the others,
it's all milk bottles and blackberries and death.
Unable to answer, I remind her of my mother.

iv

Halfway to the house my parents only half
share, remembering at last that I've left
her gift at home, we stop at a supersized 7
Eleven. Here, I wander through aisles more carnival

than convenient—all the perpetually depressed
porcelain Eeyores, pricey Precious Moments
and Pocket Dragon figurines my mother
already owns—and then, between a fossilized

rose rock bouquet and the erupting iron
acne of collectible thimbles, I see the knife.
Way beyond kitsch, it sports a handle painted
with a Marilyn Monroe triptych: Marilyn

with her skirt up around her ears; Marilyn
held (loved, strangled?) outside a bus stop; Marilyn
reclining, nude, eyes closed. Inside is a blade,
curved to fit the hollow, gentle as my mother's thigh.

XII. EX OBLIVIONE

Okay, we love the dead. But when do they stop calling?
We left a message, yes, expecting at least a token
response, but not this, not the constant carillon, ring
tones axing us open, tearing us up, interrupting
what dreams we've been allowed, spilling sleep
like a thick sick. Stew of all we thought was gone.

Late night, light loitering only in the most unkind
windows, we rise and walk. We pass our photographs,
running fingertips over lips, sometimes theirs, sometimes
our own, the taste of dust bringing back everything
that hadn't happened yet. We touch our things, old things.
Russian nesting dolls, cracked, wrapped in spider shawls.

We wind music boxes, set fire to each electronic
screen, turn the spin cycle to scream. Still, the din
will not dim what penetrates our walls, stay the steady
parade of "anonymous" of "unknown" calls. Actually,
we know them, know who's behind them. We loved them
once. Had to kill them once. Now we want them back.

The dead. The dead and all their hang-ups.

XIII. DREAMS IN THE WITCH HOUSE

> *From the direction of the shuttered room came...a curious, choking whimpering that sounded, horribly, like a child at a great distance trying to call out...*
> —H. P. Lovecraft

i

Stacked like cordwood in the corridor
two blue blondes in bloody blue gingham call
Come play with us, toss a boy their ball.

Barricaded in the black basement,
a pale, pulseless girl trowels for her mom
among mold. She's cold. She's always cold.

Another mother beelines for bedroom
anxious over some sound. Her daughter,
oozing bed barnacle, owls her head around.

He takes it, weeping, to his living room to cut
what it's swaddled in away. Whatever
it is—blastocyst, baby—it bleeds gray.

Dining room. Mess hall. Here, the new "dad" digs
in as he's dug out, set seizing, unsutured.
A sudden red flower. Baby shower.

Rooms within rooms, an orphaned agent stumbles
at last on oubliette. Child of three fathers,
she knows slaughter and, daughter to daughter, regret.

In her dreams, in his parlor, aghast over
her lover's pallor, she dreads what already
wriggles inside her, sees what it might be. Afraid.

Foxed to a closet by some badly born Shape,
all bib-alls and bad tan, the babysitter tries
a hanger. You just can't kill the Boogeyman.

Another shower. Perhaps the most
pointed. Naked desire, naked
she... Mother. Son. Carotid cutlery.

She claws her way through cupboard to secret
sect, finds black bassinet, her child, a stranger
at its side. Within, two terrible eyes.

Tricycled, triumphant, rounding the stair,
a toddler tottles his mom toward
thin air. Demon? Perhaps. Perhaps less rare.

Monsters. Children. Monsters. Parents. Home
sweet-meated home. A family sets its table,
this fable, built bone by infant bone.

Last, lingering as if lost in his own garage,
my dad watches me, his ghost, drive off
again. No movies today. No final words.
Hands hang at his sides like strangled birds.

ii

A schoolhouse shines with centimeter song, kid cackle.

Our house used to brim with birds, invariably
owls. Each screech, hoot, barn raptor, rapturously
recreated in a clash of claws and decoupage.
Macramé marauders, carnival glass carnivores.
Once, under a tacky fabric tableau—our size
six family framed in owl incarnations—
my parents came to blows over ravens and crows,
headless chick flicks, father/son horror shows.

My mom hit her head, bled a bit beneath those
six stitched pairs of eyes. Some open. Some closed.

Out of doors, on the monkey bars...one black grackle.

Morning. Dad's already abandoned the rookery
for work, sisters at school. Mom and I still
in bed. I'm supposed to be quiet, like those times
when she gets her calls. Covert conversations,
secret rings I dread like shrike song coming
through walls. And there. I hear it. Again. Again.
Mother, sleepy-angry, *Knock off that racket*, then,
What's that din? It doesn't take long to divine
what's tapped, what's trapped. A bird's gotten in,
wrestling in our vents as an angel might, with sin.

Another bird joins the first. Black blooms on the jungle gym.

One Easter my folks flocked our garage with baby
chicks, small tufts of down and dither, each one dyed
a different color—purple, red, green. My sisters
cradled them, kissed them, cooed them till they were blue.
We think the dying killed them, one by one, the color
creeping in, but I—so much younger then—I suspected
love. And when my sisters, one by one, began to leave
too, I remember holding the oldest one, afraid, alive,
saying, Is it me? So she held me back, told me to believe.
Her purple Ulster, my face framed in its down. My hand, her sleeve.

Two become four. Ravens, butcherbirds join in hymn.

The afternoon I came home, Mother at our table,
I went to the kitchen for milk, strawberry Quick,
then heard, as red bled into white, her ask,
Baby, do you know what divorce is? Dead to her
eyes, not thinking, I said, *We'll miss you.* And so
she turned, went back to her room. Later, bored,
out in the yard, I found some bird, perhaps a crow,

beating its bent wing pink against the sugared snow
and went to her. *Should we keep it, or let it go?*
I watched her stroke it, snap its neck, then swallow.

Now forty, now four hundred. More, always more birds.

My ugliest aunt. I was doing clothes when she called,
dividing darks from lights, spilling silent hills over the rest.
The call seemed to last for hours, my father saying,
No, I didn't know, and, *Even when… But we were still…*
Then, *So that's why she asked for her own apartment.*
My father fastened to the phone. Tears, Tide, dirty laundry.
Once the cycle stopped I heard the birds. My father,
eager to escape now, guessed they'd gotten in the walls. Later,
he called the landlord. They sealed our holes with plaster.
I heard them for weeks—wings, beaks, ever after.

The world? All wing now.
Feathers so dark, light hurts.
Another one comes, dives,
swerves. More, more birds.
We don't know why they come.
Rage? Revenge? Nothing
serves. Each eye pitiless.
Each crow disturbs. This
shudder, larder, murder…
Words, fucking words.

iii

Haunted houses, shuttered moons,
bed, living, dying rooms.

Playground, slayground, corridor,
cupboard, closet, killing floor.

We oscillate through halls called home
from bassinet to welcome loam,

believing we need not avoid,
yet mottled, bottled, filmed with Freud.

Shining nights of living dead,
an exorcist, eraserhead.

Alien, Damien, Halloween.
Psychos on the silver screen.

Lambs *ala* flies with hors d'oeuvre eyes...
a baker's dozen to terrorize.

Chains and stains and ceiling hooks,
wherever we're opened we're read, like books.

It all boils down to nursery,
to fear of forged longevity.

Rosemary knew. She burned with birth.
We live, that death may walk the earth.

YOUR MOTHER'S NAKEDNESS

The box I brought her home in read
affordable, something she'd never been.
The cardboard was only temporary,
thin skin to protect the red oak within.
When I removed it, what remained
stood like a minature monolith
on our kitchen table. So much smaller
than I'd imagined. Midget mausoleum.
Olbrich ashtray. Clown car coffin.
The price of admission had always been
high, so many paying so handsomely
over the years. Now, we'd been forced
to go cut rate, finding flames infinitely
cheaper. No funeral hack for her, no
sirens or escorts, no Tuff Turf, no winch.
The opening and closing alone
would have broken us. Months after,
prepping my dad's property—he too
moving on to smaller quarters—
we realized she'd been cast aside, lost
for a little season. When we found her
again in the garage, in yet another box,
this one chockablock with old kettles,
old bottles, I told my sisters I'd take her,
keep her, give her space on a shelf
laden with other mother matryoshkas.
She sits there still, skull lighter, snake
skin cigarette case, half a pack of Salems
laid before her. Beer to one side, a Little
King of course. And all around her?
This house, this urn, these ashes.

RETURNING TO THE RUIN

Not that long from Olduvai we walk
the stones it put together, marking
each crude window, each doorway and type
of altar. Not so much has faded
then. An observatory, a spade
near the remains of a factory,
a shell casing, some bones. Here we find it.
Our brain. Its halves curled like brittle fists,
like twins, slap-stilled fetuses preserved
as few are ever preserved. This half
for speeches, for towers and urging.
Another for whispers and sorrow,
for dreaming. Here, it tamed tools. Here,
it molded death. From this, like Athena,
its many gods sprang—voices that bridged
the ages between primate and prophet
with sleep. One fist spoke to the other
here of bush burnings and of Babel.
Cradling a thousand virgin breaths,
a dozen or so eternal creeds, our brain
fled its own double once and named
that myth the past. This half, the woman,
bore the other from a parting of the sea.

CANA

Like wine on white linen, my sister's
passion, four-hundred African orchids,
stained the church an odd April purple.
Bridesmaids lined up like bruises near the altar.
Cousins doled out rice packets skeined in mauve.
The cake, trussed with forty gusseted
birds of paradise and a fountain
overflowing its second sweet tier, reproduced
itself in lilac pools in the church basement.

After the long walk (me, my patent whites
too tight, on the sides of my feet), after
rings, vows, beehives, boustiers and "Nearer
My God to Thee," after pennies and pumps,
the requisite garter and gardenia toss,
limburger left on the engine block,
after Grandpa saying he thought he'd stumbled
on some rich man's daughter's nuptials,
my father found he'd let the reel run out.

I was the "ring burier" that spring
when my oldest sister married the only
boy at church my mother had said no to.
We spent hours on that ungainly audio,
respooling the entire length with a pencil.
And when that didn't work, when we realized
what we thought we'd recorded had failed,
we gathered everyone together—purple,
purple to the last—and did it all again.

II

And Cain went out from the presence of the Lord, and dwelt in the land of Nod, on the east of Eden.

—Genesis 4.16

DRAWN TO MARVEL

I

Doug's dead now and I don't know how to feel.
I grew up wearing his clothes, wanting
his toys, learning to love—from superheroes
to *Star Trek*—all he loved of the world, each
wrecked and suspect mystery. I remember
the first night I saw his parents slipping him
into diapers before bed. The look on his face.
He was four years older than me. It took time
to understand his disease, how they'd given
him, all told, twenty years. And I can still see us,
tethered to that TV, two boys cut from the same
crayon, same sheen, drawing aliens. Pine Green.

A friend says regret is a grown up
emotion. I don't know. *Is* it emotion?
Is envy, surprise? In all those years of *Star Trek*,
half of what Spock avoided always seemed
like something else to me. Reaction maybe,
autonomic. Like whacking your crazybone
with a crowbar. Wasn't he only half human
anyway? And me? Staring down this worm
hole, the warp tunnel of forty, asteroids
looming in the forward viewscreen, only half
my humanity to go, well… I find myself missing
something, everything. Marvel. It's important.

Remote control dinosaurs slugging it out
under the Christmas tree. Mini Mad Doctor lab:
COMES WITH TILT-TABLE, BODY PARTS. No friends
till I was ten. But then a whole complement
of cousins. And none cool as Doug. His taste
in TV, movies, toys. Green Hornet, Green Ghost, Ghost
in the Graveyard. Late night fright festivals at Aunt
Sissy's. Contacting her dead eldest, Jerry,
with a Ouija board. The wooden swords another

cousin, dead now too, made for us. The dying
mole we found in a hole. Rock'em Sock'em Robots.
Box of rubber hearts, back of his closet, under the insulin.

So, the real question… Is there anything
to regret? The way I've treated women,
a few friends. The toys I left when I left
my first marriage. Two divorces. Adolescent
resin, Bryan barnacles. Never getting
to Egypt. Leaving a lump like a mud dobber's
nest on my Father's forehead. Missing my old
nanny's funeral, my two cousins', Doug's.
All I know is I caught myself surfing
the net today, looking for "classic" toys,
some I had as a kid, some my parents
never sprang for. I miss so many things.

Baron Karza comes with three rubber-tipped
chest missiles, firing fists (four included),
rocket pack and magno-powered joint adapters.
He can be made more monstrous by removing
his legs, his horse's head, and plugging the body
into the cavity left behind. Colonel Steve Austin
features bionic eye (wide-angle lens), bionic
arm able to lift an engine block (included).
The arm itself sports removable bionic modules
beneath retractable rubber skin. JUST LIKE YOU
HAVE SEEN ON TV! *"We can make him better
than he was before. Better…stronger…faster."*

But why? A commercial for the new
Beetle says the Sixties are gone. Now you
can buy them back. Is that what this is?
Nostalgia, not regret? Is there a difference?
Why should I give a shit about Lee Majors,
his synthetic simulacrum? Or Karza
or Kirk or any marvel whose identity lies

in being broken? Those boxing robots were made
to reassemble after rapture. Steve Austin himself
was never happy with being anything less
than whole. So why am I set on OPERATION®,
on buying it back, returning to the ruin of what remains?

Take Dr. Don Blake. Until he happened
on his hammer, Mjölnir, he was lame. The devil
that dared tights and horns, ecstatic handsprings,
death-defying tucks and rolls, no eyeholes
in his mask? Blind. Stephen Strange? Nerve damaged.
Tony Stark? Bad heart. Sergeant Fury, agent
of S.H.I.E.L.D.? One eye. And Captain Marvel
Jr. and Batgirl and Professor X and, okay, *all*
the mutants… Regret. Regret. It's not just
toys. All my favorite marvels, every hero I had—
Jerry Lewis, Gilligan, Spock, Doug, the Abominable
Dr. Phibes—none of them ever finished.

Did Doug feel alien? Do I? Is losing the past
like losing legs? Is *losing* Doug anything
like what Doug lost every day, a tad more
each time he tensed at needle's touch? I try
to imagine those last months, wondering
at the aptness of a life that dismembers itself
as it goes. Lying in bed remembering my own
lack of real loss, I imagine myself him, watch
the world shrink down to a pale green dot,
itch to scratch what can't be called, in good
conscience, human. Is this all emotion is?
Regret for whatever's left, everything that isn't?

Fourth grade. Long before the gangrene, the lost
limbs, Doug drew desire every day. I don't mean
simple sketches, a few licks of licked lead in a spiral-
bound, blue lined notebook, no, he drafted whole,
new comics—twenty pages, gutters, panel zooms,

three point perspective, dialogue balloons—the real
thing, honest, in maybe an hour. What I recall most,
though, is power, the sheer abandon of it, the way
he threw his body back and forth across his desk,
drew as if whipped from within, as if the story
had begun its beating, not on paper, but fist to fist,
as flesh, pounding out its future on his heart.

II

Diagnosed diabetic the year I was born,
    You must begin with circles, some the size
my cousin taught me to live. How to let go
    of certain change, a dime, say, two quarters.
of a lit bottle rocket, pop the tarred, dark
    In the extremities, use even smaller ovals,
bubbles on days so hot the streets boiled, guide
    a geometry of diminishing returns.
go-carts, build robots. How to skate, stilt walk,
    As you move from one arc to the next,
clock a cropped horned toad with a rock, dodge that bright
    surprise yourself with lines, connecting
blood, what shot from its eyes. How to know a hero
    absence to absence until the frame
when you saw one, tri-colored, caped, omni-identitied.
    creates a trajectory of seeming
Late nights, lacklost in Lubbock, we'd saddle up the ghost
    action that almost looks like it could live.
cycle, thumb our way through Kung Fu, Daredevil,
    The hero you have begun—this stick figure
the man without fear, Doctor Fate, Tommy Tomorrow,
    fueled by long white, graphite, eraser stubble,
Spectre, Steel Sterling, man of steel, the New
    raggedy man made up of mostly empty
Gods, Kamandi, the last boy on earth.
    space—this imagined muscle vessel,
If it weren't for the diapers, ampoules of insulin

                    well, he needs just that. Start with each
in the Frigidaire, you'd've never known. He lived
                    oblique, with the beauty of the gut.
this way, in my memory, for years. Then suddenly
                    Continue with the pecs, making sure
it's '82. They cut off his right leg. Dialysis begins
                    to look for where they connect. Don't leave
seven years later. Three-hour hauls to the hospital,
                    his breast heavy only, unable to support
three days a week, seven hours of recycling,
                    itself. Deltoid, bi-, triceps, the curdled
new blood nearly every other day. The next year,
                    ripple of all you wish to appear,
paralytic. Dead from the chest down. Still,
                    as they say, ripped…all this complex anatomy
he can drive with hand controls, ride horses
                    may require help. Perhaps you should
with a special saddle, keep his family believing
                    consult a book. If not, stop now, return
by joking, popping wheelies in his chair.
                    where you started. Take off your clothes
Then, three years before the end, bed bruises, skin grafts,
                    look at yourself, see how we all fit together.
more than seven hundred stitches, arthritis, kidney
                    Bone, muscle, blood vessel, stubble, the subtle
infection, colostomy, the other leg.
                    breaks between one undiscovered region
A sore so deep it never heals. Later, the heart
                    and another. Finished? Time now for
attacks, two of them. And hands…gone. Eyes, gone.
                    the face, the hair, shadow on the brow, under toes,
Graduated drowning; his own humors. The day
                    other assorted endowments. Finally
before he dies, strangers from Tombstone come
                    the costume. What you've been waiting for.
to take him for a ride in a covered carriage.
                    This must be perfect, new, surprising,

It is April—month the poets call cruel, flower
    able to expand in every direction. He's a symbol,
of the new millennium—when he finally says stop it,
    don't forget. He must perform miracles, he must
stop,
    be brave.
please,
    Braver still when just
just turn off
    standing. He must abandon
the machines
    mere design, drawn to what marvel he was made for.

ALCHEMY

Colored bottles lining glass shelves in the foyer,
cut glass doors letting day-lilt in to fondle each
awkward edge, each unstoppered emptiness…
I always wondered what came in those bottles.
Sconced and squat, coiffed and crenellated, clear,
incarnadine. I imagined all manner of eldritch
effluvia: banshee bisque, eau de djinn, fallen
angel urine sample. And next to these horrible
humours—near the banister, your stair, that single
helix brachiating straight to your room—a perfect
gingerbread house. Oh, Hal, I remember your house,
all gothic claptrap, Byzantine basement of terror
and delight. The sour spray of feral cats, Rock'em
Sock'em robots ready to lose their heads at the slightest
touch. I remember the treehouse out back, playing
Which Witch is Which till dark descended on us,
till I was too afraid to climb back down. Midnight
monster movies, your collection of Frankenstein
comics, whole boxes of rubber organs, electric
dinosaurs, the Vincent Price Shrunken Head Apple
Sculpture kit I coveted. Each haunted house
you made for me, for us, your younger cousins
in that brackish barn, once even in your own room.
Your room, yes, that too. Bubbling skull candles,
black light poster paint, a stolen Yield sign redesigned
to take back the night. But during the day, Hal,
during day, your rock garden, feldspar and quartzite
glowing like glass, green as grass, adrift in the sand
they'd come from. Magic shows, mime extravaganzas,
and of course your greatest gift: the baton. I recall
you one Fourth, you in your tall pom-ponned hat, batons
and machetes aflame, scratching eternity into night's
darker design. And later, Hal, still more magic, more
patterns, embroidered shirts, the reupholstering business
you began after leaving your Bible, your bible-
bloated wife, your beard, all of Oklahoma behind.
When they asked about you at your mother's funeral,

while you lay dying in that Frisco hostel, just one
more statistic in a tub full of numbers, when, just
months later, only two or three appeared at your pall,
I tried to explain haunting, the strange perfection
of flame, how it leaves nothing in its wake but the fact
that it was born, how philosophers waved it once
over stone, bone, gingered glass. Bidding them transform.

ZOMBIES

                        It's night. Hell
is full. The dead walk the earth, and you, alone
among them, still remember the heart, the comfort
of its necessary beating. Here, trapped between
mausoleum and mortuary gate, weaponless
save for perhaps your fear, you realize you
should welcome even this, the uncertain
arc of it. All stomp and rut. All ruinous gallop.

                        Like ill-loved love
dolls they come—disfigured, uninhabited, rotting
to the bone above each uncapped knee, each weeping
wound gone dry. Splintered sternums no longer
suck, fractures go unknitted. Corporate, feral,
they shamble out of the dark on feet meant only
for ossuary floor, paramedic gurney, satin
foot rest. There is the smell of licorice.

                        Sweet forget-me-not
of formaldehyde. Necks loll back and back
till scalp meets scapula, then suddenly
a head whips forward flashing rictal gleam,
lidless teeth, open, intent on one last tongue
touch. Stumbling forward, they close on you
as you plant yourself, pristine as a leper's
femur, in the thick of all this creeping flesh.

                        Beside a tombstone
you make your final stand. Stealing the arm, shoulder
and all, from one who may have been your father, you fend
them off for a while, waving his limb before you
the way you would a dowsing rod, a hand of glory.
Living, you tire. Fighting, you fall. Past lovers
get to you first, their mouths glorious, their gums hot.
What teeth they have rip rivulets down your shins.

                    Two naked cousins—
their skin opal, bloodless, hair pale as what is now
still left of you—tear thick, stripped steaks from your thigh.
Shock arrives. Pain subsides. Flippering up close, close
enough to see his eyes—each slack cataract
gone black with hunger—your lost uncle, broken
backed, slams your skull against a slab until it cracks
and everything, all the forms, drowse into dark.

                    Here, where it began,
the dead continue moth-like to collect,
teeth grinding mindlessly into gristle,
ghouls unspooling your two intestines
one slow mile at a time. You can only watch
as your loss expands, a viscous pool lapping
up the world beneath you, gnawing. Consumed
at last by all that you have loved.

LIPS

They began, of course, the first half of the horror
show's theme song. *Michael Rennie was ill the day
the Earth stood still...* Nearly as large as the screen
they inhabited, they seemed more tease than terror,

more O than E, more you than I. *But when worlds
collide, said George Pal to his bride...* You know
the rest, know all about rice and toast and time
warps, fishnets and fuck me pumps, lonely lights

over at the Frankenstein place. Me, I was still
a virgin, but everywhere I looked…lips. Yours,
your friend's, your friend's gay lover's. Before I left
that night, I would taste them all. I'd walk out

of the theater, cross the line of a lone
picketing protester god-shod in Jesus
walkers, his passion jacked up on training
wheels, and enter another kind of darkness.

I would remember you, your lips, the cave
I never left, forever. How you whetted me for all
that followed. How the tongue, like wind, breezes
past each entrance, and how, after, the mouth freezes.

THE BARN

When we packed it all up—gently used empty spirits
boxes, cardboard hives designed for Big Beauty
tomatoes, mildly odiferous milk crates, newsprint,
poster tubes, strapping tape—neither knew this
would be our last move together. Nor did we
suspect what little we would see of it again. Last
I looked, just before we left, it still stood there,
in the barn, on the farm that's no longer a farm,
stacked back and back against the black rafters
where digger wasp and wood bee nest. Two
marriages and twenty years later, I still say "Barn"
when asked where X is. It's not like I give a shit
about the oak table or the waterbed or the tie dyes.
But my first robot, Rom? My remote control R2D2?
Moon base with rocket launcher and lunar lander?
Barn. My nearly complete set of Micronauts,
Biotron, Baron Karza, and Acroyear included?
Barn. First printing of my first bad book?
Barn. Videosphere, lava lamp, fully articulated
black knight in made-to-scale, pre-pieced armor?
Barn. Original remake of *King Kong* movie poster,
two hundred Big Little books, *Bomba the Jungle
Boy*, records, comics, oh God, the comics…
Barn. At this point, it could be anything. Rock'em
Sock'em Robots, Quick Draw McGraw bedsheets,
magic books, smoking skulls, happier sisters.
A mother who doesn't scream Mrs. Bates, father
who doesn't have a mind of winter. No bad
students, no bankrupt bookstores. Walter Cronkite
again. Frank Frazetta again. Bradbury. Bradbury.
More poems, more wine, cats that don't die. All of it
waiting, there in that barn, there among the wood bees.

THE HORDE

It's never a question of what they will take.
They will take most everything. No, the question
should be, for you—there behind the balustrades,
your face a dim accompaniment to the stone
that frames such frail, harried features, a cheekbone
grown cold, cozied against your granite bastion
as you watch them storm up from the palisades,
all hair and hubris—what will they leave behind?

When they come, and they always do, you will want
to have taken care to have watered the crepe
myrtle, the oleander. You will find
yourself reshelving old books. Thick, gilt...
no matter. There is only so much proof.
You will want to have loved enough.

IF ONLY YOU COULD SEE WHAT I'VE SEEN WITH YOUR EYES

Candle flies fill the air between our deck
and the dying elms, those twisted boles that lean
like green gossips along our black back fence.
Green. Everything is green, even in this dark.
The sky after storm. The last breath of moon.
Lightning bugs luring their mates. Each lazy
light, each night's lost lover hovering, female,
flickering over ground that slowly vanishes
beneath what pattern their ache makes.
I know the names: lampyridae, noctiluca,
glowworm. But their fire, the hypnotic
blink of abdomen, abdomen, abdomen
shining then winking out, almost as if in
sequence, makes them matter more.

Imagine the stars in three dimensions,
across space, across time. Suns coalescing
out of gas. Lights, lights, and then whole
worlds wheeling about them, worlds only
Rilke—perhaps his orphaned Orpheus—could
cobble out of lyres. Stars coming into being,
living, breathing, dying. Imagine us, left
to the linear, to time's temerity, seeing only
this one or that one go up like candles, Rome.
One, only one, every so many thousand years.
Now imagine the universe time-lapsed, like
those monkeys grown old in an instant. Ape now,
muscle now, now bone. Look at all that love, all
those civilizations on fire. How they light our way.

Or look at you, woman. I still see you there, back
of the class, red hair blazing fluorescent. You
came in every day, as alive as the stories you told
of your electrocution. How you almost died, rose
again. I admired you, desired you, pretended
you didn't move me. But the others knew, students
who said the sparks were so strong, none dared pass

between. Your father, electrician. Your license,
LIVEWYR. Your touch—that one night, handing
back some sci-fi movie you'd borrowed—green
with fire, bioluminescence. You were still my star
pupil then. Untouchable, brilliant. But student? No.
From then till now, here on our shared step, you've taught *me*
to see. Distance, darkness. The light that burns between.

LOVE POEM, HONEST

You're the zombie let loose in a romance,
the Voldemort part of my soul.
Torquemada to my Tchaikovsky.
Kevorkian rock and roll.

My dreams are your Russian experiments,
my sunsets your palate of pain.
All the parts I'm ashamed of and camouflage,
you decorate. Cake in the rain.

You navigate—tone, torque, and tenure—
each cataclysmic climb,
weighting my all with the wax of my fall,
the arch of each waxwing spine.

You've given me unperturbed suburb,
a beautiful son, a wife,
a noontide astride a huge yard, deep and wide,
weeding and cleaving life from life.

I stop here, if just for a moment,
look back on this place that we live in,
thinking, *God, oh my God, this is everything
never fathomed, never forgiven.*

Dear wife, you're my tower
of weakness, the temple of my disbelief,
the heavenly gates of damnation,
the hunger that renders relief.

You make the halt heal, every flaw flame,
my very brokenness croon.
You're my green Gatsby party, my mean Moriarty.
You are my Thulsa Doom.

MS. MARVEL

I

At 120 miles per hour, cloud-clad, wingless
as a tern turned into wind, she plummets
from plane to plain, from prop wash to prairie
plush as if her life has always been this, just this
rush, this rapture of cirrus, cirrostratus, this flood
no broken breathing can bear, air's unspeakable summit,
one long, lush sigh begun from between other
and ether, mother and mother's thigh, from blood-
bronzed breech, out, out into oxygen's unspent
reach, eventual eclipse, from God's syllabled lips, falling,
only ever falling from delivery to development
to drop zone to *this* in one undone breath, one living
lung lilt, one freighted wait for the next exhalation
after earth's insistent gasp, death, life's inspiration.

II

After all, earth's insistent grasp on death is inspiration.
And gravity? That too. It pulls her like lodestone
to all that terrifies, all that might make her mean
more than some terrible, brief spark. Before this one
run at the grave, she has explored ocean, the open
road, New York's naked runways, husband, husband,
but nothing compares to riding nothing but wind
and adrenaline down to well under a mile, then,
in an ecstasy only *almost* final, blowing her chute
for a slow ride back to everything, like the horizon,
made of hope and heartache and Kansas kitsch,
yellow roads, yellowed odes, memory's wicked bitch.
No, nothing below seduces like sky. Not Oz, not Tam O'Lin.
Only the rip cord's whisper untwists her: pull, don't pull, hammer in.

III

Only the rip cord whispers when it twists her, the pull
of hammering in no longer as luscious as knowing
now she might. Her canopy backwards, towing
her into spirals she might otherwise envy, the whole
earth auguring edgewise, nothing where it should be...
She considers cutting away, giving in, letting air
do what air does, breathe her back to the drop, the near
side of tomorrow, but no. That would be too easy.
Reserve... Nothing in her has ever had it. Her cells
might be behind, but she wants this, wants to ride
the danger down, so, reversing everything (all
that was right, now left, all that is left...), she, the tide
wind, both push her past what she believes she's missed, a tower.
Then, confused, lost in crossed lines, she touches power.

IV

Confused, lost in crossed lives, she once touched
power. Carol Danvers, that old avenger Ms.
Marvel. It all comes back in a flash. The whiz
bang of comic clarity, three-color conviction, each
inch of electric metaphor. "This female fights back!"
read the corner cover slogan. And she did, twice.
From the moment that ancient alien device—
a Kree psyche-magneton machine—blew her back,
melded her makeup with another Marvel, she
was destined to survive, destined, while alive,
to fight first her own body *then* others, to imbibe
what power she had taken in, be healed by what peeled
her to the skin, begin again. Not easy, then, this calling.
Heroine made whole only by half, flying to keep from falling.

V

Her one, her whole made only half, flying to keep
from falling, she lands with no feeling below
the belt. 12,500 volts has entered her like sleep,
cut off each impeached leg from her brain and blown
back out through the back of one hand. Drawn
to the metal of altimeter, up through the body's
cold count of curious minerals, the current still fawns
about her frame, kissing here, caressing there. *Ladies,
Gentlemen, behold our* true *Lazarus*, she thinks. Fuck
Prufrock, fuck Plath. *This* is who the Eternal Paramedic
comes for, crypt unzipped. She, whose arteries and tendons
won't return, whose thighs have embraced abandon.
Parachute, power lines, pound of flesh, the haze of praise.
She *will* come forth. She will continue to cook for days

VI

As they came forth—s/heroes, ingénues, crooks, all dazed,
all touched by power—she devoured. Twixt Christie
and Ripley's, after the latest *House of Mystery*
but before *Young Love*, she channeled each static-crazed
stalwart, each latest legend in a rush to combustion:
Miss America—mad-lab machine, accident, lightning.
Lightning Lad (later Live Wire), his brother, the menacing
Lightning Lord, his sister, Lightning Lass—all well-done
by shocking beasts back on Korbal. Captain Marvel, the teen,
Mary, Marvel Junior... A whole *chez* Am, family of flash.
Then, of course, Flash himself—chemicals, cloud crash.
And how about Hulk (okay, bombarded, but electric green),
Electro, Shocker, Black Adam, Black Lightning, at last the fantastic...
For her, now, recalling not but appalling *pop*, the message? Classic.

VII

For her, now, recalling no longer appalls. That pop,
the message of the electric? Primal, Jurassic.
Like Danvers, Carol, our heroine of the Direct
Current, like every marked marvel, universal cop,
she has learned to live without it though it galls.
Today, glorious in her skin, the skin still calls
for silk, for the body's blind euphoria when it falls,
more risk, crisp infinity, less civility of walls.
Most don't recognize, note the subtle seams.
They see, see only woman, not the world's dreams.
Even I—tangled in her body, its terminal extremes—
touch only the tiniest part of power, know she means
more than this, this harrow of heat that takes me, all lunges,
plunges, burns and turns me into her falling, falling lungless

toward awe, toward ah   ah God
                                                    at 120 miles

                              per

              hour
                       cloud-clad   wingless.

III

And he said, I beseech thee, shew me thy glory...
And the Lord said, Thou canst not see my face:
for there shall no man see me, and live.

—Exodus 33.18, 20

WORLDS IN COLLISION

And then to us, as even to the best of worlds,
there came another. Under the churling sconces
of a sky scott full of what looked like anything
but itself, beneath whirling wind screws of light none
of us had half a mind to understand, we stood
looking up, watching it come the way the Tlingit
must have watched the clipper ships of white men sink
into their lives.   I'd never seen the northern lights—
never will, now—but this is how I'd been told to
see. The waves of what must have been a battle
between one magnetic sheaf and another,
the polar, bipolar war of magnum roiling
even then beneath our feet and played out up there
above us, the shower of unholy, beastly
simple weather, and only the slightest shift
of mantle... None of this seemed so odd as that disc
(one not even our last best dreamers dreamed existed)
suddenly usurping the moon.   Sister shadow,
brother bark, wanderer in the rime-dark deep of night.
Kennings. Metaphors. The language of having nothing
else to say. As that new body approached, becoming
as it came less heavenly than even Trinity,
its cloud, words finally failed us and we ran. Stumbling
between goodbyes, between cargo and cult, ourselves
and what we'd cobbled into craft, we found nothing—
not stone knives or interstellar drives, not Verdi
or Vermeer, all temperature Cheer, gold-vermilion
gush, orange Crush, flies, ryes, stale moon pies—nothing
fit the orbit of that ark like what little we saved
of our lives.

TALISMANS

At ten, all I wanted was a whistle,
some bubblegum googaw the local Safeway
kept reliquaried inside a pay-per-view bell jar.
I would have sold every comic I owned for that
whistle, the one I imagined magic, vast of voice,
preternatural of power, shrill enough to fill
even the dead ears of the bullies who tamed me,
taught me my place, the least likely path home.
For years, after school, I found the real
kissing sneaker heel, grass beneath, dire demands
above. *Suck my cock, kneel.* Darjay or Junior
or Robert Ford looming over me like the lost
sense I once had of myself. How many times
did I pray for that power to grace my lips
(the label said sonic after all) and then, like
human timber, every axed asshole falling away?

Of course, this is how I'd been *taught* we would
fall, freed from greed to rule and rebuild,
fresh from this flesh of grass and grief, revival
tent and sneaker print. I imagined it, night
after night, revisiting the shame, remembering
how easily I'd believed. Too like the times
the noon whistle blew and my skin rose again,
each hair saluting the certainty of Rapture.

At eleven, it was a kung fu ring. At twelve,
Spider-Man pajamas, my special Superman
shirt. At fifteen, first love. And at sixteen
and twenty and twenty-seven, always some
sure thing, mystic talisman, love's luckier
charms. Something to prize and idolize, to promise
myself to. Something to ensure the space between
me and the coming cataclysm would never close.
Always the oldest of hopes, that when the skin
grows slack and the final black fact arrives,
the spirit will rise. No angry Oklahoma wind,
no whistle, no plain. No bullies to beat me to oblivion.

THE DEATH OF ORPHEUS

From the forest catacombs they came,
naked, anointed only in wine,
hair wild with karst thorn and almond
bark, bits of dried blood. Breasts small and large,
heavy, pouty, prim, all heaved forward,
nipples hauntingly erect beneath
packed mud cracked through with crimson
and mixed with brain. Pudenda hung, wealed
and wanton, below the curves of bellies,
licking out into light from the uncut
thickets they'd grown themselves. Like locust
they swarmed from between the dark ribs
and boles of rockrose and black myrtle
and attacked. Orpheus, lack-locked and longing
for the one he'd just lost, fell easily before them.

The Maenads, the mad women of Thrace,
loved Bacchus—ale arbiter, orgasm's
architect, god elect of every secret
sect, king of the blind dance—but since the new
man, this other, gentle lover, trespassed
their forest, they'd found another fool
for fawning. From the moment he arrived
he rebuffed them, returned them to scrub and scree
like packing souls back into the black
sack the flesh becomes. Perhaps it was his voice,
the songs he sang wandering womanless
among the hills that drew them. Perhaps
the passion he sang of having lost, even this,
the very absence of love lured them,
but when they finally embraced the one
who had turned once too often, the one
who, in turning toward, had somehow turned
away, was it they or he who grasped the end first?

The arms were easy. Pinched off like eyes,
potato eyes. Next, legs. A bit more gnawing
at the crotch. Cock? Tossed. Balls greedily devoured.
Ribs opened, each brittle petal peeled back
to reveal that dead, red sweet. In the end
there was only his mouth moving, still
singing, his maw as fathomless as the Hebrus
they heaved his pieces into, as the sea
he no longer saw. By the time his head
came to rest on Lesbos, the Isle of Woman,
he had become that absence he so craved,
become song, singer, lyre, the death he'd wished
returned to life, the life he never lived
except outside it, kneeling at its yaw.
The women who found it buried the head
deep, but not before they'd memorized the words
they heard, what music he made of silence.

What was it then? The singer or the song,
lyre or lunacy? What drew his death
down on him? Orpheus, alone, seduced
by the sound of his slim shadow, his music
caressing every tree, every unrent rock
torn between forms, between what is known
and what is only ever imagined…
When he reached down into the darkness,
set death's own worm turning, plucked beauty
from the abyss and climbed back out
trailing only an idea behind him,
the notion of what he loved gathering
its graveclothes as if against that chill the real
recognize, yes, but too late, did he know
then that his call, his attempt to return
her to the world was doomed from the first note,
that his song and hers could never claim
the same key, the one he'd fretted it into?

Nothing loves the lyric like the poet,
and since this is all he had, all anyone
has—the shape, not the thing—she went
back into the black where he had no claim,
back to where she'd always been, that place
he could not touch. This is no different
from what he'd made his habit—assuming
he understood what he wanted, thinking
he could call his suspicions his own. No,
nobody knows how to bring just one
unbroken thing into the world, and no one,
not even the gods, can send it back
if it isn't already going. The song
has never loved the singer.
The song loves itself, playing us
like the lyres we are as we float
on ceaselessly into the grave.

THE RIGHT TO BE FORGOTTEN

The European Court of Justice tells us
we have this "right" now. The right to be
forgotten. *I* want the right to forget.
I want the right to forget my father,
the man he once was, how scared he must
have been down the length of those hours,
those fifteen long hours he went missing.
I want the right to forget how he forgot
where he was, where he was going, how
to get home, how to grieve *his* father
whose grave he found there in Carnegie
Oklahoma, two tanks of gas from his house
in a field near another, older house, the one
he grew up in, a mound of earth rising
to meet feet that somehow knew what
his mind had lost. I want the right
to forget my mother and the voices
she sometimes hears now, the little
dead girls she talks to, the mad bombers
and Jeffrey Dahmers who want to make
a wasteland of Wal-Mart where she thinks
she still works. I want the right to forget
how earnestly I cried over losing my second
wife, how badly I treated the first. I want
the right to forget Los Angeles, the terrible
fear I felt there, so lonely, so poor, so
stupid. I want the right to forget all
the crazy women I wound up with,
the one who dreamed her dead dog
under the bed, the one who let her other
self break up with me. I want the right
to forget High School, the year I broke
up with myself, stalking my ex and her
skateboarder boyfriend, hoping to find
them fucking in the back of his yellow
Beetle. I want the right to forget Junior
High, all the bullies who demanded I suck

their dicks. I want the right to forget how
I fooled my father into believing I liked him,
enjoyed riding bikes with him, when what
I wanted was to get away from our bachelor
pad, the apartment where the bullies lived.
I want the right to forget that moment
my mother asked me, "Do you know what
divorce is," and I said, "We'll miss you."
I want the right to forget that dear, doomed
dick who's been hurting others ever since
he punched his sister in the stomach one
Christmas, who later made his mother cry
with his poems. I want the right to forget
every way I've ever hurt the ones I love. And
that me? He wants the right to be forgotten.

SEA OF TRANQUILTY

It happened
in space,
in orbit,
among dust,
among rocks,
using craft,
having left
Earth's berth
to find purpose,
to be more,
and we planted
flag, footprint
on a world
not our own.
But there's pictures.
There's rocks.
There's tape.
Well, it's lost.
But the images…
the audio,
the science,
the story,
the import.
Humanity…
Faith.
Our reach.
We made it
up and out.

Or not.
Or not.
Or back lot.
Perhaps not.
Papier-mâché.
Craft? okay.
Good sense,
all pretense,
all ruse.
Don't confuse.
Nothing, nyet,
horseshit.
Made of cheese?
Oh, please.
What? Of Yeti?
There's confetti.
Not today.
You don't say.
Are fake,
a mistake.
Says we couldn't,
says we shouldn't.
Minimal.
Animal.
Now you're talking.
Knucklewalking.
Yes, up.
No, doubt.

THE LOST WORD

Whitman died chasing Champollion, seeking
grammar for God, a uniform hieroglyphic.
American answers for Egyptian enigmas.
Still, he found no stone, no Virginia Rosetta.
Dead language. Dead union. Leaves of grace.
From Humboldt's humble hunch to Grimm's
lautverschiebung to Chomsky's mysterious miracle,
we seek first clause, the name of he who names.
And Adam? No. What logic was ever uttered
in Eden? Do not eat, said the seraphim. Do not
partake of this knowledge, *this* that would make
you obey. You should not know what *not* is not
for you. Do not eat. Do not, and burn with desire.
Do, and burn with despite. Boëthius in his cell.
Socrates on his couch. Aristotle, Aristarchus,
Beauvoir, Baudrillard. All sought solace in symmetry.
Argument, artifice… Art in the desert of the real.

Suppose Saussure got rhetoric right. "Here,
look for where it begins, where the saying
starts, posit unknown from known and watch
the sign signify what you never intended.
Publish what you never published, argue
what others only ever *said* you said. No,
begin again without yourself, with yourself only
signified, referent to nothing. *Imagine* nothing.
Argue even after death, after silence, *always*
after that. Provide, provide." Bakhtin knew,
and Barthes, Eco and Foucault. There is no
general course, nothing but everything outside
the cave, the lingering linguistics of longing.

Velikovsky wanted something out of nothing
too. Wanted Jupiter, Dyu Pitar. God. Father.
This and Venus, fully formed, from his brow.
Wanted it so much he made it out of math.
Offered equations proving the planets Pong.

Spat forth from storm and eye, his imagined
proto planet zigzagged through our solar system,
passing sister Earth, parting the Red Sea,
dropping manna. None of this, of course,
happened. Except it did, on paper, on papyrus,
among the numbers in the many means of God.

So. Geometry also. Not just grammar or logic,
rhetoric or arithmetic. There are always
other roads. Remember, Escher drew us
into the plane. Made the stairs that take us
where all stairs should go, bridged our absence
where nothing becomes something becomes
nothing again. Dimensions divided, angles
arbitrated, hand drawing hand etching images
of enzymes and ants, geese and gravitas,
humanity and infinity, the romance of reflection.
We are the shapes that shake us. We shape
the shaped *us*. But having no end, owning no
original arc, we lose ourselves in the labyrinth,
looking, always looking, mounting the stair, modeling
Möbius, moving across the great girth of earth's grid,
plotting, rising, falling, always falling, into formula.

Finally there is Mozart, Mozart and Drake.
We could mention so many, humanity's long
lineage of making meaning of the moans
the moon makes spinning seas up from darkness,
spitting us forth, calling us home. Musicians
and astronomers, all the madmen and the maimed.
All trying to mutter the music of the spheres.
Mozart plucked it down to play as performance.
Drake made math out of why we might pluck
at all. Mozart gave voice to the wolf, to the hour
when the stars speak, when our souls seek
anything but silence, everything *as* silence.
Drake defined the size and scope of said silence.

Said likely we have never been alone. The number
of communicating civilizations in the galaxy?
The number of other souls? The sheer volume
of possible answers to our ancient arrogance,
our quixotic questions? The name of the name
of the being who best knows God?

If the number is even a fraction of a trillion—
the number of stars we see most close about us,
this galaxy, this home… If the number is even
the smallest part of the 300 sextillion stars
saturating the larger *unseen* scope of sky,
all we know and don't know… If they too
have planets, which they will, if they too
have seekers, which they will, if they too
have Huygens and Hawkings, Shakespeares,
Saussures, golems, Grimms, Mondrians
and Mozarts and Masons, which they will,
they too will have sought all that is not.
All that is. They too will have waited
for the word. Carved in bone, in sandstone,
in gnarl and gneiss. They too will have hollowed
out caves at their version of Karnak and Callanish,
Jericho and Jeju Island, Turobong and Toposiris.
Temples. Always temples to the word.

But what is it, this word we seek, this emptiness
nothing seems to satiate? What I AM?
What I AM NOT? From Chauvet to Chartres,
from Tan Tan to Berekhat Ram to Teotihuacán,
nothing becomes the something we desire.
Desire becomes reason to reanimate all matter
that matters. Golem. God particle. Golden
record. We put our words between ourselves
and that which we cannot name. Holy of holies.
JHVH. INRI. ACTG. SETI. Letters, always letters
on the face of the deep. Christ carving his word

in dirt, a code to keep the craven at bay. Cain
on his knees, at the watering hole, washing,
washing a sign unutterable, a stain that will not
not but stay. A rabbi, entering the temple, God's
name aflame on a tongue he dare not wag.

And the temple at Karnak. A name spoken
to bring back the sun. And Loki screaming
it, eternal, in the dark, in pain, beneath
the brunt of everything earth. And Yeats turning
and turning to nothing in his nodding Tower.
Bradbury channeling childhood from the stars.
Melville, scribbling, spotless as a lamb. Eliot
shoring up ruins. Rushdie and Lessing
and Lovecraft and dear dead Dostoyevsky.
Everyone, Clemons to Clarke, Dante
to Dickinson. Faulkner, last man on this doomed
dark rock. Einstein, Ellison, Edison, Morrison.
Quill to kinetoscope, pumice to papyrus,
Guttenberg to Gettysburg to Googled Gliese.

We have made our marks, made our signs,
sent them sailing, soaring, failing into the night.
What words? All words. All but the one
we have sought. All but the right word, the one
we lost before the rest. The name, the name
of the one who made us, laid us brick by brick,
set us on the level, encompassed our corners,
rounded what was rough, set square that which
strayed, the one who tamped us, tested us,
smiled upon us, deep as the deepest temple.
The one who beveled all that cannot be
altered. Altar, Psalter, stair, infinite author
of our inner path. Origin of everything more,
everything ore. Article. Particle. Core. More,
more light. At the center of all, before that first,
last, best disaster. We seek it fast. We seek
it faster. We seek our Master.

RAISED IN THE BLOOD

She led me, her sheep, behind the piano
to show me, I suppose, how she was made.
How, even at eight, we already shared
that human greed to enter into difference.
There is only so much we cannot want
to know, only a tiny window between
leaving the bough and bursting to seed.

So she took my hand during Bible drill,
drew me away to one of the few corners
we had learned to vanish in, a spot secluded
as any elementary paradise can be—
our Sunday school god, Mrs. Martin, too busy
speaking words into light—and there, she lifted
her dress. Funny, I remember the color
of her wool sweater, sweet sorghum, her skin, just shy
of sorrel, the frayed, beige eyelet edging the leg
bands of her panties, what cool candor
the interest of her eyes took in finding
something similar in mine, the unsettling
sobriety that infected her fingers
as they caught the corners of her underwear
and sheared them down. The down, fine, fresh, unshorn
that pelted her legs, stopping just above
the knee, what rapt confusion I felt mistaking
her navel first for something deeper, and then—
just as mons broke free from that slow, cotton
horizon—the first kittenish skittering
of my own sex at last recognizing corduroy.

I remember all this, the verses we were
supposed to be learning, *Genesis, Judges, Ruth,
Song of Songs*, all the ones who had led me to this
place. Linda, Laura, my own sisters even,
the once I'd caught them dancing in their skin,
bold bottoms turned to me, shaking, dreaming
they were alone. I remember the medicine

bottle choked with eraser tops, how I'd labeled it
Love Potion to trick Diane Green into kissing
me. Duane and Jimmy dropping drawers at one end
of the playground crawl-barrel as I peeked in
at the other. The "marriage machine" I'd labored
from a Vicks inhaler and a broken car
antenna. All this is as crisp as the marquee
cut diamonds in my mother's many wedding rings.
But what I thought I saw that day, what my first
vision of entry, exit, another world
meant to that eight-year-old stoic finally
and utterly alone behind a badly tuned
piano is no clearer to me now than it was
the next Sunday when a church volunteer
took me aside—just one in a long line of lost
children—to ask, *Have you let the Lord Jesus
into your heart*, and all I could say was, *Yes,
yes*, raised already in the blood of the Lamb.

CROSSING THE SNAKE

> *People who know me love me and to love me*
> *is to know that I am not evil.*
> —E. Knievel

We have gathered here today to witness

    The truth. Witness how the truth can never die.

  In the back of that Baptist church, beneath

a true hero ladies and gentlemen,

    Here, in the one book that doesn't lie, here,

  the portrait of a man painted perhaps

a man some name the Moses Lake

    in the midst of war, between one boy dying

  too soft, a few pews back from my Sunday School

Messiah. Our own truck stop troubadour,

    and the next… *This* is the end of all we call

  teacher, his lessons still loose in my head

everybody's Easy Rider. Leather Elvis,

    lies.

  like prayers, I was only half hearing

the Gap Glider, Air Orchestra... The one,

                Jesus. Living word. The word inerrant,

       our preacher, my attention divided between

the only...

             ineffable. Exemplum of sacrifice. Both

     the sermon, and another, taller tale:

Evel!

             judge and jury. He who must sit astride

    Evel.

Here he is folks, riding

           that last, pale horse, the throne from where

     He was going to jump Snake River Canyon, leap

in on his trademark wheelie. They say

           he will know us, mark us saved, or pitch us

    across that gap on a machine more mock rocket

he can ride 'till the top end runs out of oil.

             into that lake where the fire is less what we see

    than cycle. Secretly listening to

Today, Evel will be attempting

                    on TV—all napalm and naked lust,

         what was promised, the spectacle of a lifetime

something no one, not even Neil Armstrong,

                  murky microcosm of what we are—

         simulcast on radio, only one dutiful ear

what *no* astronaut would try. This is more

                  than the accumulation of everything

         tuned into church, the other plugged, prodigal,

dangerous, more complex than any leap

                  we never should have been.

         hoping to catch some glimmer of greatness

ventured before.

                  Turn with me now

         from this man who wasn't afraid to fall,

From here, at the end of that closest ramp

                  to Genesis, the second chapter

         to stake life on limb and break every bone

Evel will soon be boarding his Sky

                    with the strange change some of you

          imagined… Oh, how I wanted that…

Cycle. Be patient folks. The fun is only

                noticed in passing. See how the story

         that beginning, something startling

just beginning.

              starts again. Some have called this a discrepancy,

        to jump start a life I hadn't begun,

…

            a flaw, a gap in the text of the Word.

      and I suspected most everyone else

…

            But *I* say this isn't some Sumerian

      listening, even those around me, needed the same

…

            miracle of mix and match. Holy is not

Evel.

Friends and neighbors, the wait may be

                a guessing game. It means what it means.

        To my parents, I must have looked like I was

over. It looks like…wait…

            It isn't about interpretation or

      listening, learning how texts collide,

no. Evel has already taken up position

            finding the proper historical context,

      paying true attention to the lesson

in the cycle. You can hear the engine

            it's about faith, about knowing the Word

      I would learn in full only later.

racing right now. The smoke you see from the fuel

            is the font from which we spring, and the Word

      That story we told, still tell, ourselves,

is really steam. Evel says you can even drink

            says we were made, and we fell, and we became,

      that story of the garden, of one woman who set

it straight. This is the newest baby

            well, what we are.

        the human race on the road to ruin

in Evel's arsenal of modern machines,

                Woodstock, Watergate,

         and the man who listened, who took

the next generation.

                  a sick nation stuck in a war we can't win,

      the apple, her body, the man who took

What you see before you,

                at war with all we wouldn't dare recognize as

       us out of the garden and down the path

that which you will witness today, is like

                ourselves. And we're losing, we are lost

      to mortality... I would finally see

Jesus on the Sea of Galilee,

                in this gap, the space we imagine behind

      that *story as minor madness, metaphor,*

like Moses parting the water...

        the words. What isn't there. False gods, false

    as a necessary lie, the Snake itself,

...

        needs, a void we've made of what we want

    but not just yet. First, I had to understand

...

        to believe we need to fill. But brothers,

    a man who could raise himself from the dead,

...

        sisters, there is no gap but the Snake,

    who was, if only when broken, us.

Sorry about that folks. There seems to have been

        no valley but the shadow, no leap

    We didn't know. Not then. No more than

a bit of trouble with the cycle,

        we need to make, no leap but the leap

    we know now. But we, I... I wanted to be

a few simple problems, but let us return to

        our Lord made from that hill of skulls. The gap

    that man, someone who had no fear,

the scene of the action. Evel.

        is in us, not outside of us, in the flesh,

    no need for gravity, no need for any

Man of the hour. Here he is once more.

        not in the Word. Christ took up his cross

    law, really. He could break anything.

Even the great canyon before him

        and closed that gap. His wounds, our wounds,

    Thirty-three bones. The lower back, twice.

means nothing. This cycle and this man…

        were healed when the curtain tore, when his hands

    Crushed coccyx, concussions, fractures.

about to achieve the impossible. The world

        ripped, when his side split and the clouds cracked

    Plates, pins, the memory of land grown large,

is only waiting for the flag-man's signal.

                and the gap between us and God—the one

        lush as paradise, anxious to close

The sky…. Wait, that's it! The sign!

            we opened when we opened the garden

        that final ground. This was his time, his day,

Yes, he's moving, he's in the air…but… No, the chute

            gate—closed behind us both. This is his body.

        and it never really mattered if he made it

came too early. He's going down. Evel has crashed

        This, his blood.

    across.

in the canyon.

THE RIVER

Somewhere on the border of Oklahoma
we traded positions in our sleep, woke,
and watched the sun undress the morning.
Later, when a beetle struck the truck
window, you wiped rainbow from your face,
turned to me, shaken, still looking
for signs where they had been
the year before: *Beware the Illinois
River monster—THIS MEANS YOU.*

Three days canoeing on the river,
we spoke little of graduation, even less
of ourselves, spending our arguments
quickly, artlessly, remembering how
to steer. After a night on the shoals
of a severe bend, sleeping bags dug
into sand like shallow graves, we woke
half-soaked and warmed together
over an open fire and stew.

The second leg was strong from a break
in the current, and that night night
leaned on our shoulders as we opened
ourselves a generous share of the bass
we carried in our chests. It seemed so small,
the stock we had taken. In each other
we could see vast visions trapped in amber,
every empire we could imagine, all
the time we'd never have to remember.

Near the end, our words, moths courting
cold light, wandered too close, the rat-eyed
embers in the fire pit played shadow tag
across our faces, and fresh ash clabbered
in the throats of our eyes. On the border
of three o'clock, black shapes—hoofed, horned,
ruminant—passed over us like thunder, and dreams

of that passing woke us from our sleep. Dark
prints, evidence of immanence, let us know…

It could have gone on forever.

THE RIFT

July 2011, Kennedy Space Center

Our final craft arises from one blue
and sinks into another we call true.
Deep calls unto deep, the Psalmist states,
suggesting that our blood is like the straits
we nod beside when sounding out our souls
from here, the edge of space, these restless shoals
where ships have launched toward the blackest sea,
where mothers, husbands, wives upon this lea
have watched the ones they love let go of Earth,
trajected into something too like birth,
that airless ocean where we once accreted
from waves of dust and absence, superheated,
molded, brought to being out of flood,
like Love herself from salt and foam and blood.

We've shuttled past this garden, spent our spoor
outward, always outward, always more
to fight that feeling that we may be less,
to find a balm for Gilead's unrest.
We do not want to be here in the dark,
alone, without the hope of other ark.
We sow the upper air with lenses, mirrors,
reflecting on our existential terrors.
No, this is not the first, the last Atlantis.
We stand upon the strand like Marinatos
who stumbled on the ruins of that city.
Plato wrote about it, wrote with pity.
He also wrote of love, its rift, its scars,
of all we seek when we seek out the stars.

ACKNOWLEDGMENTS

I would like to thank the following venues in which some of these poems have appeared:

Harvard Review	"78"
Ridded With Arrows	"Fatherland"
Love Craft	"Love Craft"
Weird Tales	"Necronomicon"
Cimarron Review	"The Promise"
	"Returning to the Ruin"
	"Talismans"
Dissections	"Drawn To Marvel, Part I"
	"Lips"
The Cresset	"The Barn"
Drawn to Marvel	"Drawn To Marvel, Part II"
Paddock Review	"The Rift"
Poems Dead & Undead	"Zombies"
Farrago's Wainscot	"Worlds In Collision"
Cutthroat	"The Death of Orpheus"
Barely South Review	"Sea of Tranquility"
Philalethes	"The Lost Word"
Yale Review	"Raised In the Blood"

Thanks to Alfred Corn, Bruce Bond, Tania Runyan, and William Pitt Root for their generous belief and praise. Thanks to the Newman Art Department for returning me to my art, to the Theology and Philosophy Departments for reminding me about faith, and to Michael Austin who stood up for my soul. Thanks to my early readers, particularly Leah Maines and Bill Coleman, for bringing a dead book back to life. And finally, thanks to Curtis Shumaker, Clive Revill, and the Culver City Foshay Lodge for recording "The Lost Word" and eternally tending the light.

Bryan D. Dietrich is the author of nine books of poems and co-editor of an anthology of superhero poetry. He has published poems in *The New Yorker, The Nation, Poetry, Ploughshares, The Paris Review, Prairie Schooner, Harvard Review, Yale Review,* and many other journals. Finalist for the Yale Younger Poets Prize, as well as the Walt Whitman, Pablo Neruda, and Bram Stoker Awards, he has won the *The Paris Review Prize*, the "Discovery"/ *The Nation* Award, a Writers at Work Fellowship, the Lord Ruthven Award, and has been nominated for both the Pushcart and the Pulitzer. Bryan is Professor of English at Newman University in Wichita, Kansas.

www.ingramcontent.com/pod-product-compliance
Lightning Source LLC
Chambersburg PA
CBHW032235080426
42735CB00008B/864